Writing Research Reports for Social Studies

McDougal Littell
A HOUGHTON MIFFLIN COMPANY

Evanston, Illinois ▪ Boston ▪ Dallas

With minor exceptions, this book follows the style for documentation set forth in the *MLA Handbook for Writers of Research Papers.* Documentation style for some recent technologies, including on-line computer services, has been updated.

Printed in the United States of America.

ISBN 0–618–03695–4

3 4 5 6 7 8 9 – DCI – 04 03 02 01

Contents

Writing for Assessment

How can you succeed on a social studies test? Of course, you have to thoroughly understand the material you have studied. Sometimes, however, understanding the concepts isn't enough. To do well on many social studies tests, you must be able to convey your knowledge clearly in writing. This section of *Writing Research Reports for Social Studies* can help you succeed at test time.

Assessment Types

First, you should identify the type of assessment you are dealing with. The comprehension questions and chapter reviews in your textbooks are one kind of assessment. Tests are another. Tests come in two basic forms: classroom and standardized.

Classroom tests. Classroom tests are those given regularly by your teachers. Like textbook questions and reviews, classroom tests usually require not only objective answers but also longer written responses.

Standardized tests. Standardized tests are those given to students across the country and scored against national norms. Many standardized tests, such as the ITBS (Iowa Tests of Basic Skills), Stanford Achievement Tests, and TerraNova tests require you to analyze social studies readings. As you will see, the same skills that help you to analyze and interpret essay questions can also help you to analyze and interpret these readings. Some standardized achievement tests, such as the CEEB (College Entrance Examination Board) tests for social studies and for history, also include essay sections.

The rest of this chapter looks at the types of questions you are required to answer on many social studies tests.

> " To do well on many social studies tests, you must be able to present your knowledge clearly in writing. "

Questions Based on Graphic Devices

Many social studies tests ask you to interpret or complete graphic devices, such as time lines, tables, graphs, and flow charts. When interpreting such graphics, be sure to note what information the questions are asking you to interpret. Sometimes a graphic device includes information that is not necessary to answer the questions. This is included to determine whether you are able to identify the important information.

Time lines show the order of events, such as historical incidents and discoveries, as well as eras and trends. A time line is divided into segments, each representing a certain span of time. Events are entered in chronological order along the line.

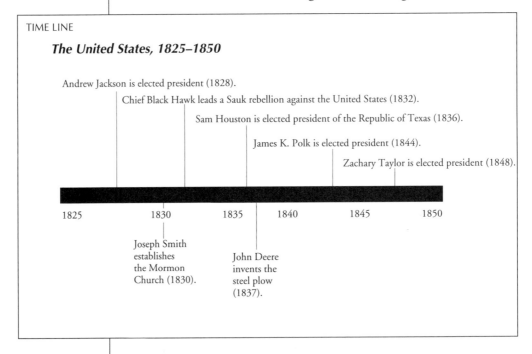

TIME LINE

The United States, 1825–1850

Andrew Jackson is elected president (1828).

Chief Black Hawk leads a Sauk rebellion against the United States (1832).

Sam Houston is elected president of the Republic of Texas (1836).

James K. Polk is elected president (1844).

Zachary Taylor is elected president (1848).

1825   1830   1835   1840   1845   1850

Joseph Smith establishes the Mormon Church (1830).

John Deere invents the steel plow (1837).

To interpret or complete a time line, take into account not only the dates and the order of events but also the types of events listed. You may find that events of one type, such as wars and political elections, appear above the line, while events of another type, such as scientific discoveries and cultural events, appear below it.

Tables show numerical data and statistics in labeled rows and columns. The data are called variables because their values can vary.

Workers' Average Monthly Salaries, 1830–1850		
JOB	YEAR	MONTHLY SALARY
Skilled worker	1830	$45
Laborer	1830	$26
Teacher, male	1840	$15
Teacher, female	1840	$7
Farmhand, northern	1850	$13
Farmhand, southern	1850	$9

Source: *Historical Statistics of the United States*

To interpret or complete a table, read the title to learn the table's general subject. Then read the column and row labels to determine what the variables in the table represent. Compare data by looking along a row or column. If asked, fill in any missing variables by looking for patterns in the data.

Graphs, like tables, show relationships involving variables. Graphs come in a wide range of formats, including pie graphs, bar graphs, and line graphs.

PIE GRAPH

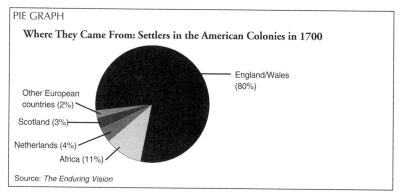

Where They Came From: Settlers in the American Colonies in 1700

Source: *The Enduring Vision*

BAR GRAPH

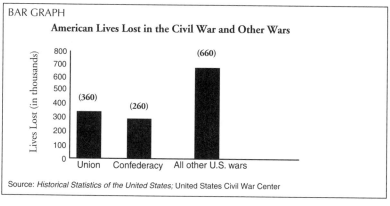

American Lives Lost in the Civil War and Other Wars

Source: *Historical Statistics of the United States;* United States Civil War Center

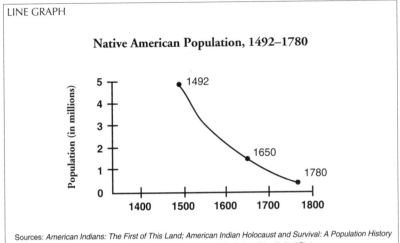

LINE GRAPH

Native American Population, 1492–1780

Sources: *American Indians: The First of This Land; American Indian Holocaust and Survival: A Population History Since 1492; A Concise History of World Population; Historical Statistics of the United States*

To interpret or complete a graph, read the title to find out what the graph shows. Next, read the labels of the graph's axes or sectors to determine what the variables represent. Then notice what changes or relationships the graph shows. If asked, fill in any missing variables.

Some graphs and tables include notes telling the sources of the data used. Read these notes carefully. Knowing the source of the data can help you to evaluate the graph.

Web diagrams and related devices, such as cluster and tree diagrams, show relationships between ideas or events. Details, examples, or related incidents are shown on branches extending from a central idea, event, or theme.

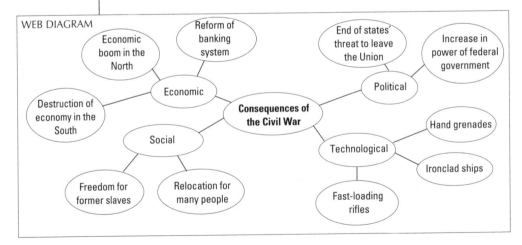

WEB DIAGRAM

4

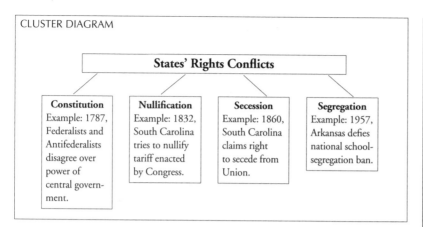

CLUSTER DIAGRAM

States' Rights Conflicts

Constitution	**Nullification**	**Secession**	**Segregation**
Example: 1787, Federalists and Antifederalists disagree over power of central government.	Example: 1832, South Carolina tries to nullify tariff enacted by Congress.	Example: 1860, South Carolina claims right to secede from Union.	Example: 1957, Arkansas defies national school-segregation ban.

To interpret a web or cluster diagram, first identify the central concept. Then classify the entries that branch out from it. For example, they may give details or examples supporting a general statement, causes or effects of an event, or characteristics of a person, an issue, or a historical period. If asked, complete the diagram by supplying entries in appropriate categories.

Flow charts show processes that have several steps. Each step may include more than one possibility. To create or interpret a flow chart, you can use the devices described in the Writing Tip at the right or invent similar ones of your own.

Writing Tip

In many flow charts, ovals stand for starting and stopping points; diamonds, for decision points; and rectangles, for possible choices or actions. Arrows show directions of movement.

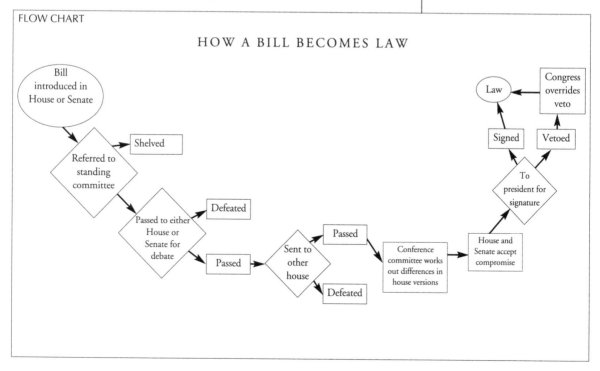

FLOW CHART

HOW A BILL BECOMES LAW

To interpret a flow chart, read the title and find the starting and stopping points. Follow the arrows to trace the steps in the process. Be sure to note all the possibilities at each decision point.

Developing your ability to interpret graphic devices will help you correctly answer assessment questions based on them. You can also use simple graphic devices to organize and present information in your answers to other questions, as well as to provide additional facts and data in your answers to short-answer and essay questions.

Short-Answer Questions

A short-answer question is one that requires a one- or two-sentence response. Keep in mind the following guidelines for answers to short-answer questions.

- **Use specific names, dates, and figures whenever possible.**

    Sample question: What does the pie graph on page 3 show about settlers from England and Wales?

    Too general: It shows that they made up almost all of the colonial population in 1700.

    More specific: It shows that they made up 80% of the colonial population, while settlers from other countries made up 20%.

- **Respond in complete sentences; avoid sentence fragments.**

    Sample question: Why did Cabrillo initially fail to discover San Francisco Bay?

    Fragment: Because of fog.

    Complete sentence: Cabrillo sailed past San Francisco Bay without seeing it because of a heavy fog.

- **Make your responses brief but thorough. Rely on precise nouns and verbs rather than vague terms.**

    Sample question: For what invention is Samuel F. B. Morse best known?

    Wordy and vague: Samuel F. B. Morse was a person who did many important things in his area of communications and made major kinds of advances in learning about the telegraph.

    Brief and precise: Samuel F. B. Morse is best known for his invention of the telegraph.

Whenever possible, respond to short-answer questions before you tackle essay questions. Short-answer questions ask for facts and details; they help you recall some of the specifics you will need in your essay responses.

Essay Questions

Essay questions require longer, more detailed writing than short-answer questions. One secret of success in answering them is good planning. Don't just jump into writing. Stopping to organize your thoughts before you write can pay off when your test is graded.

Budgeting Your Time

Believe it or not, on a timed test the clock is your friend. Look at the total amount of time you have for the essay portion of your test. The average middle school student can write half a page in about five minutes. Estimate how much you will be able to write in the allotted time, and then plan your responses. Give yourself a few minutes to quickly analyze each essay question, or **prompt,** and plan a response. In addition, leave yourself several minutes at the end of the test to edit and proofread your responses.

Analyzing Prompts

Keywords in essay prompts tell you which writing strategies to use in your responses. The list of strategies and keywords on the next page can help you analyze prompts and plan effective responses.

Writing Tip

When you answer an essay question on a test, you may find it helpful to think of the process as a shortened version of the writing process outlined on pages 11–12.

Keyword in Prompt	Tasks	Writing Strategy
explain, discuss, explore	Make an event, a process, a problem, or a relationship clear and understandable. Include examples and reasons.	explanation
identify, show, tell about, what is/are	Explain the distinguishing characteristics of a subject or the meaning of a term. Use specific details.	classification (identification, description, or definition)
compare, contrast, discuss similarities and differences	Show likenesses and differences. Support your points with details and examples.	classification (comparison and contrast)
analyze, who, causes and effects, examine, show how, explain why, in what way(s)	Show causes and effects or break a subject down into its parts, showing how they function and relate to the whole. Use facts and examples.	analysis
trace, summarize, outline	Give a short description of an issue, an event, or a sequence of events. Leave out minor details.	summary
evaluate, pros and cons, in your opinion, in your judgment	Present your judgment on an issue, an event, or a historical or political figure. State your criteria, and evaluate the subject on each point.	synthesis (evaluation)
interpret	Consider the significance of a subject and explain it in your own words.	interpretation

Planning Your Response

Main points. For an essay response, your planning must be streamlined. Take into account the writing strategy suggested by keywords in the prompt, but don't try to make a complete outline or a detailed cluster diagram. Instead, jot down a quick list of the main points your response will cover. Number them in the order in which you plan to discuss them. Plan to devote one paragraph to each main point. You might also want to jot down important dates, statistics, and names so that they will be available as you write.

It's a good idea to turn in your planning lists along with your response. Even if you don't quite have time to complete your response, your lists may show your instructor that you know the material.

Thesis statement. Write a thesis statement that sums up the main idea of your response. Your thesis statement can include words from the prompt, as in the following example.

Prompt: In what ways was Abraham Lincoln's presidency unique?

Thesis: Abraham Lincoln's presidency was unique in three main ways.

Or your thesis might be a general, one-sentence answer to the prompt—in effect, a summary of the response you plan to write.

Thesis: Abraham Lincoln was a brilliant leader in a time of terrible crisis for the United States.

Keeping your thesis statement in mind as you write can help you shape your writing.

Writing Your Response

Introduction. A one- or two-sentence introduction is fine in an essay response. Your thesis statement can serve as a one-sentence introduction. If your introduction consists of more than one sentence, be sure that one of the sentences states your thesis.

Body. Devote at least one paragraph to each of your main points. Use transitions, such as *for example,* to show how these points are related to your thesis and to one another. Pack your paragraphs with as many relevant names, dates, and statistics as

"When taking an essay test, you don't have time to rewrite your work, but you can still edit it."

possible. (In some essay tests, the number of facts and statistics you mention directly affects your score.) If you lose your train of thought midway through your writing, glance at your planning lists to get yourself back on track.

Conclusion. As with the introduction, a one- or two-sentence conclusion is fine. This may be a restatement of the thesis in different words. Remember that your conclusion should leave your reader with a clear understanding of your main idea.

Editing Your Response

When taking an essay test, you don't have time to rewrite your work, but you can still edit it. Read your work and check it against your planning lists, to be sure that you have included all important information. If you think of things to add, write them neatly in the margins, using arrows to show where they should be inserted. Use arrows, as well, if you want to move sections of a response.

Finally, proofread your responses, correcting errors in spelling and mechanics. Make your corrections as clear as possible: use a single line to cross out each error, and write the correction above the crossed-out material. No one expects test responses to be without revisions, but make changes neatly, turn in your responses, and congratulate yourself on a job well done.

Completing Classroom Assignments

In social studies classes, you are often required to explore your own thinking in essays, book reports, and reviews. You may also be asked to explore history by creating primary materials of your own, such as interviews, oral histories, and historical narratives. This section of *Writing Research Reports for Social Studies* offers guidelines for such written assignments.

Essays

Years ago, the principal meaning of *essay* was "to try." Today, *essay* more commonly refers to a piece of writing that explains facts and ideas. To write an essay is, in a sense, to try out your thinking. When you write an essay, you will go through three main stages—prewriting, drafting, and revising and editing—though these are not steps that you must complete in a set order. You may return to any one at any time.

Prewriting. In the prewriting stage you explore your ideas and discover what to write about. The lists of questions and suggestions on pages 47–49 can help you choose a topic. Other techniques for finding an essay topic are group brainstorming, freewriting, and making a cluster diagram. When you have selected a topic, note your initial thoughts about it before doing the reading and research you need to help you understand it.

Drafting. This is the stage at which you put ideas on paper and allow them to develop as you write. Decide on the focus, or thesis, of your essay, and then create a list of main points and details that support your thesis. You may find it useful to arrange your material in an outline (see page 66). Do any more research you feel is necessary, and then write your first draft.

Revising and editing. In this stage you improve your first draft. The changes you make will usually fall into three categories: revising for ideas, revising for form and language, and proofreading for mistakes in spelling, grammar, usage, and punctuation.

> " You are often required to explore your own thinking in essays, book reports, and reviews. "

Some of the changes you make may be inspired by the suggestions and comments of a peer or classmate.

The specific characteristics of essays vary, but most strong essays have the following features:

A focus on one major idea, or thesis. In the opening paragraph, identify the focus of your essay in a way that makes readers want to read on.

Several main points explaining the thesis. In each paragraph of the essay's main section, or body, cover one main point related to your thesis. Start a new paragraph whenever there is a shift in your ideas or emphasis.

Enough specifics to support each main point. Make sure that the specific facts, statistics, and examples in each paragraph support that paragraph's main point.

A clear train of thought. Arrange paragraphs in the most appropriate order, and try to make the links between them clear. One way of doing this is with transitional words such as *on the other hand* and *as a result.*

A conclusion summarizing the main points and the thesis. In the concluding paragraph, tie all of the main points together. You might restate your essay's thesis here.

Essays of Analysis

To **analyze** something is to break it down into its parts and examine the ways in which the parts are related. You might analyze congressional committees, examining their relationships to one another or to Congress as a whole. You might analyze a primary source, examining how it shows the influences of the time and place in which it was written. You might write a **causal analysis** of a historical event, examining the relationship of the event to its causes or effects.

Planning an Essay of Analysis

Make notes of facts, examples, and data that are related to the topic of your analysis. If you are analyzing a parts-to-whole relationship, you might construct a web diagram (like the one on page 4) to help you visualize the relationship. If you are analyzing a primary source, you might list characteristics and examples

The following are examples of assignments for essays of analysis:

• Analyze how the system of American government strikes a balance between too much and too little central power.

• Cite passages of the Declaration of Independence that were influenced by demands of the American colonists, and explain how each reflects a demand.

• Explain the relationship between the Mexican authorities and the American settlers in Texas.

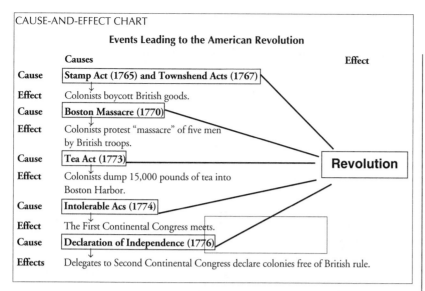

CAUSE-AND-EFFECT CHART

Events Leading to the American Revolution

Causes   Effect

Cause   **Stamp Act (1765) and Townshend Acts (1767)**

Effect   Colonists boycott British goods.

Cause   **Boston Massacre (1770)**

Effect   Colonists protest "massacre" of five men
by British troops.

Cause   **Tea Act (1773)**   **Revolution**

Effect   Colonists dump 15,000 pounds of tea into
Boston Harbor.

Cause   **Intolerable Acs (1774)**

Effect   The First Continental Congress meets.

Cause   **Declaration of Independence (1776)**

Effects   Delegates to Second Continental Congress declare colonies free of British rule.

in a cluster diagram (like the one on page 5). For an analysis of causes, try a cause-and-effect chart.

On the basis of your planning notes and your diagram, write a thesis statement that sums up, in a single sentence, the major idea of your essay.

Sample Thesis (Parts-to-Whole Analysis): Indentured servants played a major role in the economy of the Jamestown colony.

Sample Thesis (Analyzing a Source): N. Scott Momaday's "A First American Views His Land" shows what other Americans can learn from Native Americans.

Sample Thesis (Analyzing a Cause): The colonists could not have become independent of Britain without the aid of other European countries.

Then list the main points that your analysis will cover. Consider how you might best organize your material. For example, in an analysis of causes you might first state a cause and then explain its effects, or you might first present an effect and then examine its causes. Sometimes you'll want to describe a chain of cause-and-effect relationships. The organization you choose will depend on your topic and purpose for writing.

Writing an Essay of Analysis

Introduction. Let readers know what you will analyze and how you will analyze it. Stating your thesis is one way to accomplish this.

Body and conclusion. Write a paragraph explaining each of your main points. Use transition words such as *because, as a result, in the first part,* and *in the next part* to make relationships clear to readers. To help readers understand your ideas, include facts, data, and examples from your planning notes. You might conclude with a restatement of your thesis in different words.

Writing Tip

The following are examples of assignments for essays of interpretation:

• What are some advantages and disadvantages of a strong central government?

• In what ways was the Lewis and Clark expedition important to the expansion of the United States?

Revision Checklist—Essay of Analysis

• Have I made relationships clear? Where might I add transitions, facts, or examples for greater clarity?

• Have I avoided oversimplification? For example, have I taken into account multiple causes and effects?

• Are my paragraphs in an order that makes sense? Might any sections of my essay be more effective if I moved them?

Essays of Interpretation

To **interpret** something is to consider its significance in the light of what you know. You might interpret facts or events by writing a **hypothesis**—a guess that you can test—about their implications. You might interpret a primary source by exploring the viewpoint it expresses. You might interpret an issue by presenting the arguments on both sides and examining the assumptions that they are based on.

Planning an Essay of Interpretation

If you are writing an essay in which you advance a hypothesis, you might conduct a survey or poll to test your hypothesis. If you are interpreting a primary source, you might fill out a web diagram (like the one on page 4) to help you identify viewpoints and find examples. For an argument, you might try a tree diagram similar to the one shown on the following page.

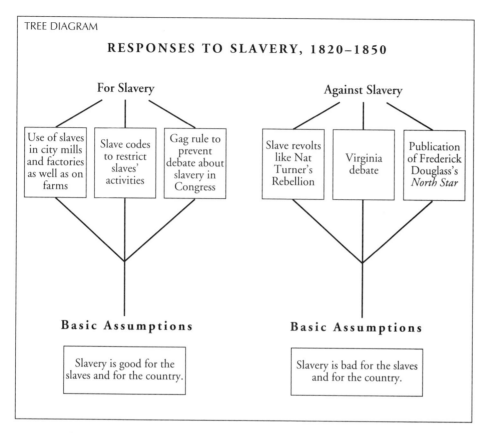

TREE DIAGRAM

RESPONSES TO SLAVERY, 1820–1850

For Slavery

| Use of slaves in city mills and factories as well as on farms | Slave codes to restrict slaves' activities | Gag rule to prevent debate about slavery in Congress |

Against Slavery

| Slave revolts like Nat Turner's Rebellion | Virginia debate | Publication of Frederick Douglass's *North Star* |

Basic Assumptions

Slavery is good for the slaves and for the country.

Basic Assumptions

Slavery is bad for the slaves and for the country.

On the basis of your planning notes, write a thesis statement expressing the main idea of your interpretation.

Sample Thesis (Hypothesis): Without the many slave revolts in the early 1800s, the Civil War might not have occurred.

Sample Thesis (Argument): Acts for and against slavery between 1820 and 1850 kept the issue alive in America.

List the main points that your essay will cover, and then choose the best way to organize your material.

Writing an Essay of Interpretation

Introduction. In your opening, identify the source, issue, facts, or events that you will interpret. Then present your thesis.

Body and conclusion. Use the body paragraphs to support your thesis. Include specific data and statistics from your planning notes. If you have advanced a hypothesis, state the facts on which you based it, and tell how you tested it. If you are interpreting a source, provide examples to illustrate your points. If you are interpreting an argument, be sure to give equal weight to both sides of the issue. Explain the underlying assumptions on each side, and support your statements with factual evidence or experts' opinions. You might close by stating the significance of your interpretation.

Revision Checklist—Essay of Interpretation

- Does my reasoning make sense? Should I take into account other options and possibilities?

- Have I made my reasoning clear to readers? Where might I add transitions to improve clarity?

- Have I included enough evidence? Which points might I strengthen by adding more facts or data?

Writing Tip

The following are examples of assignments for essays of classification:

- Compare and contrast Thomas Jefferson's and Alexander Hamilton's ideas about government.

- Define the term *mass production* and describe the effects of mass production on the economies of the North and the South in the early 1800s.

Essays of Classification

To **classify** things is to sort them according to their characteristics. You might write an essay of **comparison and contrast,** examining the similar and differing features of two concepts, events, or historical figures. You might write an essay of **definition,** explaining the features of a thing or concept so that readers can identify it and understand it.

Planning an Essay of Classification

If you are writing an essay of definition, a web diagram (like the one on page 4) can help you sort out and group your subject's features. To organize your thoughts for an essay of comparison and contrast, try making a Venn diagram similar to the one shown on the next page. Write similarities in the area where the circles overlap and differences in the nonoverlapping parts of the circles.

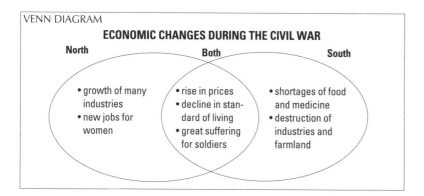

VENN DIAGRAM

ECONOMIC CHANGES DURING THE CIVIL WAR

North — Both — South

North:
- growth of many industries
- new jobs for women

Both:
- rise in prices
- decline in standard of living
- great suffering for soldiers

South:
- shortages of food and medicine
- destruction of industries and farmland

Write a thesis statement in which you sum up the overall idea suggested by your planning notes. You can then look over your notes or diagram for facts and details that support your thesis.

Writing an Essay of Classification

Introduction. Specify what you will compare, contrast, or define.

Body and conclusion. To compare and contrast, you can choose either of two organizing patterns. In an essay organized subject by subject, you first discuss one subject and then discuss the other, pointing out similarities and differences. In an essay organized feature by feature, you address each feature in turn, showing how the subjects resemble or differ from each other in terms of that feature. In either case, help your readers follow your ideas by using transition words such as *on the one hand, on the other hand, similarly,* and *in contrast.*

Revision Checklist—Essay of Classification

- Have I made my subject clear at the beginning of the essay?

- What is my organizing pattern? Have I kept it consistent? Have I used transitions to make it clear?

- Have I included enough examples, facts, and data about each feature? Where might more details strengthen my essay?

In a definition, present the features of your subject by category. You might devote one paragraph to identifying characteristics, another to uses or effects, and another to background or origin.

You might close your essay of classification with a summary of your points or a restatement of your thesis.

Essays of Synthesis

To **synthesize** ideas is to put them together in your own way. You might synthesize evidence in an essay in which you draw a **conclusion** about a historical event. You might synthesize your thoughts in an essay of **opinion** about a social issue. You might synthesize judgments in an essay explaining your **evaluation** of the solution to a historical, political, or social problem.

Planning an Essay of Synthesis

In planning a synthesis, you might start with a question such as "What do I think about this?" or "What do these facts add up to?" When you have chosen a topic, start gathering information. You might make notes of observations, memories, or research. The more information, the better. You can't base a valid conclusion, opinion, or evaluation on just a few details.

Try putting into words the question that triggered your synthesis. Then write a one-sentence answer based on your planning notes. That answer can serve as your thesis. List several reasons (again, based on your notes) that support it, and choose the best way to organize your material.

Writing an Essay of Synthesis

Introduction. You might open with the question in your planning notes. You can then present facts in the body of your essay, "adding them up" to arrive at your thesis at the end. A second option is to start with your thesis and present supporting reasons in the body of your essay.

Body and conclusion. Be careful not to assume that your viewpoint is the only valid one. Present the evidence on which you have based your conclusion, opinion, or evaluation. You might explain each reason in a paragraph, first stating the reason

The following are examples of assignments for essays of synthesis:

- Which regions benefitted most from the Columbian Exchange—the Americas or Europe, Asia, and Africa? Support your answer.

- Do you think that liberty or equality is the most important right a government should offer its citizens? Support your answer.

and then providing details from your notes to back it up. In an evaluation, carefully explain the reasons for your opinion.

Close your essay by summing up your thinking. If you have not yet presented your thesis, do so in your final paragraph.

Revision Checklist—Essay of Synthesis

- Have I stated my thesis, either at the beginning or at the end of my essay?

- Have I included enough details to support each generalization that I make? Where might I add more facts or statistics?

- Have I explained my thinking clearly, taking into account other viewpoints?

Book Reports and Reviews

At times you may be asked to write reviews of or reports about history books, biographies, or other works of historical interest.

Planning a Book Report or Review

Take brief notes as you read, view, or listen to the material you will respond to. You might note your favorite parts, parts that puzzle you, and parts that you disagree with. Afterwards, ask yourself questions to help you analyze and evaluate the material:

- Whose point of view does the work present? Which parts reveal the point of view?

- What might the work's purpose be? Which parts reveal the purpose? What is the author's, artist's, or composer's thesis?

- What are the most and least effective aspects of the work?

- What might readers, viewers, or listeners learn from the work?

Writing Tip

Simply stating your personal feelings about a book is not enough. You need to support your statements with explanations and references to the work.

19

Review your notes and decide on a thesis that you would like to present in your response. Write your thesis as a single sentence. Then list the main points you will use to develop or support your thesis.

Writing a Book Report or Review

Introduction. In your first paragraph, identify the material that you are responding to. Name the author, composer, or artist. To help your readers, provide a summary or brief description of the work. You might also state your thesis in your opening paragraph.

Body. Devote at least a paragraph to each main point. Support each point with details from your planning notes—including your own responses—and with examples from the work itself.

Conclusion. If you haven't stated your thesis in the first paragraph, do so in the conclusion. Sum up your judgment of the work's main ideas and the way they are presented.

Interviews

One excellent way to come to appreciate the value of primary sources is to create some yourself. When you write interviews, oral histories, and historical narratives, you gain first-hand insight into other time periods and viewpoints.

An interview is a gold mine of information about someone's personal experiences and ideas. For some social studies assignments, you might interview living people. For others, you might write imagined interviews with historical figures.

Planning an Interview

The following guidelines will help you plan an interview.

Make an appointment with your subject if you are conducting a real interview (rather than writing an imagined one). Ask the subject's permission to take notes or photos or to make an audiotape or videotape. Practice with your equipment before the interview.

> " An interview is a gold mine of information about someone's personal experiences and ideas. "

Learn about your subject's life and knowledge. If you are interviewing an activist or a government official about an issue, for example, learn enough about the issue to ask intelligent questions.

Establish a focus for your questions. In what aspect of your subject's life are you most interested? List questions that focus on it. Avoid questions with yes-or-no answers. Instead, start questions with "Tell me about . . ." or "How did you . . ." or "How do you feel about . . ." Consider sending your questions to your subject ahead of time to let him or her think about them.

Conducting an Interview

Bear the following guidelines in mind when you are conducting your interview.

Start off on the right foot. Arrive on time. If your subject hasn't seen your questions, explain the kind of information you're interested in learning about. Then begin with a friendly, open-ended question that will help you and your subject relax.

Sit back and listen. Let your subject do most of the talking, but be interested and involved so that he or she will be encouraged to go on. Feel free to follow up on ideas that are not on your list of questions. You can always come back to your list later.

Wrap it up. If your interview is to end at a certain time, keep an eye on the clock. Thank your subject, and leave promptly.

Writing an Interview

Introduction. In a brief opening, introduce your subject and provide background information for your readers. Mention the setting—the date and place—of the interview.

Body. If your interview is short, write up the whole conversation from your notes or recording, editing out only *uh*'s and *um*'s. You can use a question-and-answer format:

Q: How did you first become interested in politics?
A: I don't think I ever *wasn't* interested. . . .

If your interview is longer, start by writing out only the parts that seem most important. Then, include other parts that add necessary details. Be sure not to change the meaning of your subject's message. You might write "bridges" in which you summarize material you have not included. Enclose bridges in parentheses so that your words won't be mistaken for your subject's.

Conclusion. A quotation from your subject can be an effective conclusion. You might also summarize your overall impression of the person.

Check your interview for accuracy. If possible, submit your draft to your subject for his or her approval.

Oral Histories

To create an oral history, you interview an eyewitness to a historical event, an era, or a specific way of life. You then present your findings as a **narrative**—a story—told in the eyewitness's own words. The interviewer usually plays a less important role in an oral history than in an interview.

Planning and Recording an Oral History

Follow the general interview guidelines on pages 20–21. Your goal is to get your subject to recall a specific event, era, or way of life. Ask questions that will encourage him or her to give lively details and explanations.

Writing an Oral History

Introduction. Write a brief opening that introduces your subject, identifies his or her background, and states the date of the interview.

Body. If your subject uses language in a special way, don't "correct" it when you write your oral history; dialects and speech patterns are part of history too. Organize your oral history as an ongoing story. You might present your subject's memories in chronological order or in the order in which your subject recalled them during the interview. Include your questions only if they make the story clearer.

When preparing questions for your interviewee, you may find it helpful to focus on specific subject areas, such as early life, school days, social life, work life, home life, and the technological changes the person has witnessed.

Conclusion. You might want to conclude your oral history with your subject's closing words. You could also end with your own summarizing comment about your subject.

Historical Narratives

A **historical narrative** is a description of a particular historical event or issue. It may involve firsthand reporting, as in an account of a political rally in which you participated, or it may involve research and imagination, as in an account of a day in the life of a young person in colonial America. Even a narrative that comes out of your imagination, however, must also contain facts.

One format used for historical narratives is the **monologue**—a speech in which a person reveals his or her thoughts and feelings about an event or issue.

Planning a Historical Narrative or Monologue

Think about the goal of your narrative or monologue. If your work will be imaginative—if, for example, it is a monologue by a historical figure—ask yourself whether your primary goal is to present historical information, to "get inside" a character, or a combination of the two. Because a strong narrative often includes sensory details, you might find it helpful to fill out an observation chart for the events your narrative will describe. List details relating to all five senses.

OBSERVATION CHART

SENSES	Sight	Hearing	Smell	Taste	Touch
OBSERVATIONS					

> " To pull your readers in, try starting with an exciting event. "

Introduction. To pull your readers in, try starting with an exciting event. You might, for example, describe a sign-waving demonstrator at a political rally. Include details of time and place to set the scene. You could write from the first-person point of view, using *I, me,* and other first-person pronouns.

Body. Write about events in chronological order. Include transitions that clarify chronological relationships (such as *at first, later, meanwhile,* and *finally*) to keep your readers on track. Use sensory details from your observation chart to bring events to life, and add your own feelings and thoughts where appropriate. In a monologue, use language suited to the speaker and to the situation.

Conclusion. Create a satisfying conclusion with a final comment on the significance of the events or issues presented in your narrative.

Writing Reports

When you write social studies reports, you must use your research skills and critical-thinking skills as well as your writing skills. This section of *Writing Research Reports for Social Studies* can help you with the tasks of writing short reports. These tasks are also an essential part of writing longer research reports.

Primary and Secondary Sources

Source materials for social studies research can range from arrowheads to encyclopedia articles. **Primary sources** are first-hand historical materials. **Secondary sources** are books, articles, lectures, and other works that interpret primary sources.

Finding Primary Sources

The field notes of a historian studying a Native American village are primary sources, as are the artifacts and interviews he or she collects. Letters, wills, tombstone inscriptions, newspaper articles, television news reports, government documents, census reports, speeches, court records, portraits, photos, journals, and autobiographies can all be primary sources. These materials, which may include eyewitness accounts, can give you important insights into historical events. To find primary sources, you might explore one or more of the following options:

- **Museums' and libraries' special collections** often include artifacts, private letters, and original manuscripts. You might examine these in person or via the Internet.

- **Your local historical society** keeps photos, documents, and other materials about your community.

> "Source materials for social studies research can range from arrowheads to encyclopedia articles."

- **Presidential records and other government documents,** available in such reference sources as *Public Papers of the Presidents of the United States* and *Documents of American History,* include materials related to historical and political events. For personal papers of U.S. presidents, you might contact individual presidential libraries or their Web sites.

- **Interviews with eyewitnesses** may be available in your local library on videotape or in back issues of magazines and newspapers. For some topics, you can conduct your own interviews; see the guidelines for interviews and oral histories on pages 20–23.

- **Statistics and survey results** are available in reference sources such as *Statistical Abstract of the United States,* published each year since 1878, and *World Facts and Figures.* For some topics, you can conduct your own surveys.

- **Historical news articles, advertisements, and editorials** can be found in back issues of newspapers, available on microforms in many local libraries. Back issues of many newspapers date to the mid-1800s. You can also search the Internet to find newspaper Web sites devoted to specific historical periods.

- **Notes and bibliographies in secondary sources,** such as the chapter notes and references in a nonfiction book, often refer to primary sources and give their locations.

Using Primary Sources

When you work with a primary source, consider questions such as the following:

- **What is the date of the source?** Was it created at or shortly after the time of the event you are investigating, or was it created years later? How might it have been influenced by the values and issues of its time?

- **Who was the author, speaker, or creator of the source?** Was the person an observer of or a participant in the event you are investigating? Did he or she have a strong point of view? Was he or she a government official? If so, did the person speak as an official or as a private citizen? If the source is a work of art, music, or literature, was its creator free to work as he or she pleased?

- **For what audience was the source intended?** A speech for a private audience may differ from a speech for an international gathering. The views of places, people, and events in a personal letter may differ from those in government records.

- **For what purpose was the source created?** Was it a campaign speech, a piece of propaganda, or a declaration to other nations? If the source is an artifact, was it for everyday use or for a special occasion? If the source is a work of art or literature, was its creator trying to promote a cause?

- **Does the source express a strong one-sided opinion, or bias?** Look for techniques of influencing opinion, such as loaded language, overgeneralization, and circular reasoning. Did the author present opinions as if they were fact? Can the information in the source be proved?

Some Basic Reference Sources

The sources listed in the tables on the following two pages are available in many libraries' reference sections and are useful starting points for social studies research.

American History

Dictionary of American Biography. 20 vols. New York: Scribner's, 1928–37. With 10 supplements to date.

Dictionary of American History. Rev. ed. 8 vols. New York: Scribner's, 1978. Supplement published in 1996.

Documents of American History. Ed. Henry Steele Commager and Milton Cantor. 10th ed. 2 vols. Englewood Cliffs: Prentice, 1988.

Encyclopedia of American Scandal. By George Kohn. New York: Facts on File, 1988.

Encyclopedia of Multiculturalism. Ed. Susan Auerbach. 6 vols. New York: Cavendish, 1994.

Famous First Facts. By Joseph Nathan Kane. 4th ed. New York: Wilson, 1981.

Historical Atlas of the United States. Rev. ed. Washington: Natl. Geographic Soc., 1993.

Historical Statistics of the United States: Colonial Times to 1970. Washington: GPO, 1975.

Official Congressional Directory. Washington: GPO. Published annually, 1887– .

Selected List of U.S. Government Publications. Washington: GPO.

Statistical Abstract of the United States. Washington: GPO. Published yearly, 1878– .

Statistical Record of Asian Americans. Detroit: Gale, 1993.

Statistical Record of Black America. 4th ed. Detroit: Gale, 1997.

Statistical Record of Hispanic Americans. 2nd ed. Detroit: Gale, 1995.

Statistical Record of Native North Americans. Detroit: Gale, 1993.

The United States Government Manual. Washington: GPO. Published annually, 1935– .

Who's Who in America. Chicago: Marquis. Published yearly, 1899– .

World History

Africa Today. 2nd ed. London: Africa, 1991.

Atlas of World History. Chicago: Rand, 1995.

Current Biography. New York: Wilson. Published monthly, 1940– .

Dictionary of the Middle Ages. 13 vols. New York: Scribner's, 1982.

Encyclopedia of Asian History. 4 vols. New York: Scribner's, 1988.

The Encyclopedia of Judaism. New York: Macmillan, 1989.

An Encyclopedia of World History. 5th ed. Boston: Houghton, 1980.

Historical Dictionary of Vietnam. By William J. Duiker. Metuchen: Scarecrow, 1989.

Kodansha Encyclopedia of Japan. 9 vols. New York: Kodansha, 1983.

The Oxford Encyclopedia of the Modern Islamic World. New York: Oxford UP, 1995.

Past Worlds: The Times Atlas of Archaeology. New York: Crescent, 1995.

Webster's New Biographical Dictionary. Springfield: Merriam, 1988.

Who's Who. London: Black. Published yearly, 1849– .

Who Was When?: A Dictionary of Contemporaries. 3rd ed. New York: Wilson, 1976.

World Facts and Figures. By Victor Showers. 3rd ed. New York: Wiley, 1989.

Yearbook of the United Nations. New York: UN Office of Public Information. Published yearly, 1947– .

The World Wide Web as a Research Tool

The World Wide Web contains millions of pages of both primary and secondary sources of information—including photos, sound recordings, and videos, as well as written materials. You can locate this information by using various search engines. The Web is a wonderful tool to help you gather information—

but remember that it's only a tool. You need to use it along with the library and other resources to best meet your research goals.

Locating Information

Here are some steps that can help you find the information you need on the Web:

- **Plan ahead.** Write research questions that tell what you want to learn about your subject. Then circle important words in your questions that you can use as search words, or keywords.

- **Try several search engines.** Each search engine has access to different pages of material on the Web. Use more than one to locate the best selection of information. Use the engines' "help" pages for assistance in focusing your search.

- **Choose promising sites.** Look for sources that include all or most of your keywords. Many search engines show how well a site matches your keywords by listing a percentage (such as 92% or 66%) in the entry. A site that ranks 75% or better is usually a good match. Most engines present the entries in order from the best matches to the worst—so start at the beginning of the search report.

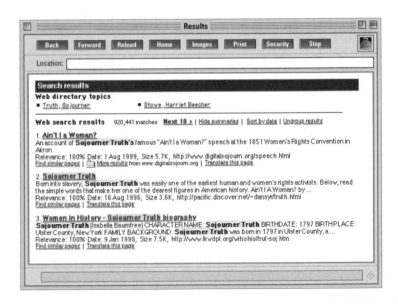

- **Explore the top sites.** Open each site and look for the name of the person who created it. Glance through the information to see if it is what you need. Look for a line that tells when the site was last updated. Also click on any links that might provide more information. Print out useful pages or save them as text files. Be sure to write down their Web addresses or bookmark them so that you can go back to them if necessary.

Evaluating On-Line Sites

Part of the reason that so much information is available on the World Wide Web is that anyone can create a Web site and register the site with a search engine. No one is required to prove that the information he or she posts on the Web is accurate, reliable, or up-to-date.

These steps can help you evaluate Web sites:

- **Check the Web address, or URL.** Sites with addresses ending in ".edu" (college and university sites) or ".gov" (government-agency sites) usually are reliable.

- **Review any information about the site's author.** Personal Web sites (for example, "Elena's Top Events in History") are usually not good sources.

- **Note when the site was last updated.** Especially when you're dealing with secondary sources, the most recent information on your subject is the best.

- **Read any on-line reviews or ratings of the site.** Many established organizations offer these. (Some search engines and educational organizations also give on-line awards for Web sites.)

Short Reports

Every time you read a newspaper article, a magazine article, or a nonfiction book, you are reading a report. The author has gathered information from various sources, analyzed and interpreted it, and used a particular format to present his or her findings. Pages 37–135 of this booklet lead you through the process of writing a research report; this section is a quick guide

Research Tip

Some encyclopedias are available on-line or on CD-ROM. Check what resources are available at your school or local library.

to the writing of short reports. The tasks discussed here, however, will also form the basis of your work on research reports.

When you write a short report, you are like a journalist writing a magazine article. You choose a topic, analyze information from two or more sources, and present the information in a way that is clear and memorable.

Planning a Short Report

The topic of a short report must be narrow enough for you to cover it thoroughly in just a few pages. You might start by reading an encyclopedia article on your topic. (Remember to read the article only for ideas. Do not just copy the text.) Notice the headings under which the topic is broken down; one of the headings may suggest a narrower topic. In narrowing your topic, you might also consider the purpose of your writing, as shown in the following table.

Broad Topic: The Growth of the Railroads in the United States

PURPOSE	NARROWER TOPIC
• To analyze cause and effect • To compare and contrast • To clarify	• How the railroads helped the country grow • Positive and negative effects of the railroads • Corruption of railroad companies

Once you have narrowed your topic, write a **statement of controlling purpose,** telling briefly what your report will cover. This statement can keep you on track as you research your topic. Later, it will become the basis of your thesis statement.

Start your research by listing questions that you hope to answer in your report. Then find primary and secondary sources of information. Check your library's catalog and reference section, the *Readers' Guide to Periodical Literature,* and the World Wide Web. Other sources include local historical sites, museums, personal interviews, and surveys.

For each source you use, make a bibliography card (see pages 58–60 for instructions and models). Bibliography cards save you time in taking notes and in creating your Works Cited list. To save more time, don't read your sources all the way through; focus only on sections pertaining to your topic.

Take careful notes, identifying the source of each. (See pages 64–65 for more on note taking.) Print out material from the Internet, jotting down the date and the source's address on the printout. For other material, use the techniques of summary, paraphrase, and quotation explained on page 61.

Organizing a Short Report

When you finish your research, review your notes. Then rewrite your statement of controlling purpose as a **thesis statement**—a sentence or two that clearly states the main idea your report will present. Then list the major points you will make in developing your thesis, and group your notes according to the points they support.

Plan the order in which you will present your points—an order in which each idea flows logically to the next. To make writing easier, jot down an informal outline in which you list your points and supporting information in the order you have chosen. If you prefer working from a more formal outline, see the guidelines for constructing topic outlines and sentence outlines on pages 70–72.

Writing a Short Report

Introduction. To catch your readers' attention, you might open with a surprising statistic, a quotation, or a memorable image related to your thesis. Include your thesis statement near the opening of your report.

Body. As you write, stay flexible. You are presenting not only information but also your own analysis and interpretations. If a new idea pops up as you write, feel free to try it out. If you can't find a way to include it in your report, you can revise your organizational plan, or even your thesis, or you can go back to your original outline. Don't forget to include graphic devices if they will make your report more interesting or understandable.

Write at least one paragraph for each point, using transition words to show how your ideas are related. Support each of your

“As you write, stay flexible.”

points with information from your research, and document the sources of all your information. For guidelines on documenting sources, see pages 87–94.

Conclusion. You might close by summarizing your research or by restating your thesis in different words. You might also refer back to the statistic, quotation, or image with which you started, briefly noting how your information shows its significance. Add a Works Cited list at the end of your report (see pages 92–94).

Multimedia Presentations

Instead of writing a traditional report, you may want to share your information in a multimedia presentation. A multimedia presentation combines text, sound, and visuals. Your audience uses a computer to read, hear, and see your material, clicking on links to move from part to part of the report. The links can be highlighted words, navigational buttons, or graphic images.

For a multimedia presentation, you need computer programs to create and edit the text, the graphics, and the sound and video files you will use. You also need a multimedia authoring program that allows you to combine these elements and to link your screens. Ask your school's technology adviser which of the following elements are available to you.

Sound. Including sound in your presentation can help your audience understand the information in your written text. For example, you might include a recording of a famous speech or one that gives the pronunciation of a foreign word.

Photos and videos. Photographs and live-action video clips can make your subject come alive. For example, you might include photographs of artifacts or images of original documents. If you have videotaped an interview, you might include clips of the interview in your presentation.

Animation. Many graphics programs allow you to add animation to your presentation. You might use animation to illustrate the steps in a process or trace a route on a map.

" Photographs and live-action video clips can make your subject come alive. "

34

Planning a Multimedia Presentation

One starting point for a multimedia presentation is a report that you have written. In such a case, your aim in creating the multimedia presentation is to make the written material more interesting by adding sound and visuals. At other times, you may plan to create your material as a multimedia presentation from the start.

When you have an idea of the material you wish to cover, you must plan how you want your audience to move through the presentation. There are two basic ways of organizing a multimedia presentation:

- in step-by-step fashion, with only one path for the audience to follow from screen to screen
- in branching fashion, so that the audience can choose what they will see and hear, selecting the order in which they will experience it

If you choose the second way—an interactive presentation—you need to map out your report in a flow chart or navigation map, as shown below. This will help you plan the links that will allow your audience to choose paths through your presentation.

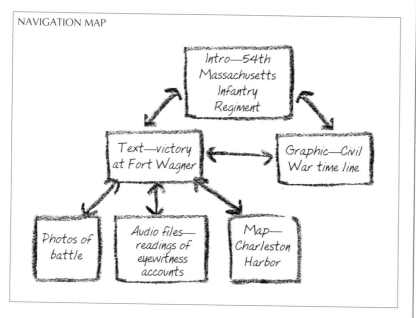

NAVIGATION MAP

CD-ROMs and the World Wide Web are useful sources of material for a multimedia presentation. On CD-ROMs you can find video clips whose subjects range from historic events to street scenes, as well as audio recordings of live performances and famous speeches. You can download photos, sound files, and video files from the Web. Be sure to keep notes on your sources.

Creating a Multimedia Presentation

After you decide on the content of a screen, you should find it helpful to sketch the screen's design. Remember to include in your sketch the links that will lead to other parts of the presentation. Use your navigation map as a guide to help you decide what links you need to add in each screen.

The first screen serves the same purpose as the opening paragraph of a written report, so make sure it gives the title of the presentation and identifies its focus. The first screen should also explain how your audience can move through the presentation. You might also add a screen or set of notes listing the sources of your information.

Writing Research Reports

The rest of this booklet is a comprehensive guide to the process of writing a research report. It leads you through all of the stages, from finding a topic to preparing the final manuscript.

Understanding the Research Report

Have you ever written a report in which you used several different sources? If so, you have already produced something like a research report. A research report is a written report that presents the results of a focused, in-depth study of a specific topic. Its writer chooses a topic, gathers information about the topic from several sources, and then presents that information in an organized way.

Writing a research report will probably be the most time-consuming and challenging task that you have ever done as a student. Don't let the size of the task scare you, though. You will find researching and writing your report quite easy if you take it one step at a time, following the guidelines in this book.

Research and the Writing Process

Some types of writing, like taking notes in class or jotting down a grocery list, are done all at once. However, most writing is done over a longer period of time. In other words, writing is a process, and it can be roughly divided into stages—prewriting, drafting, revising, proofreading, and publishing. This book will take you through the following activities in the process of writing a research paper.

> **Writing is a process, and it can be roughly divided into stages—prewriting, drafting, revising, proofreading, and publishing.**

The Research Process

- Choosing your subject
- Doing preliminary research
- Limiting your subject to a specific topic

The Research Process (cont.)

- Finding an angle and writing a statement of controlling purpose

- Preparing a list of possible sources (a working bibliography)

- Taking notes and developing a rough, or working, outline

- Organizing your notes and making a final outline

- Writing your first draft

- Revising your draft

- Writing the final draft, with a complete list of works cited

As you work through the next few chapters, you will come to understand more clearly what makes up a successful research report. For now, read the sample research report on the following pages. Then answer the questions that follow it.

Holzer 1

Jenny Holzer

Mr. Mills

History

14 April 2000

                The Second War for American Independence

        America had struggled through the Revolutionary War
and finally won its independence from Great Britain in
1776. The fight for independence was not over, though. On
June 18, 1812, the United States again declared war on
Great Britain. Understanding the causes and the effects of
the War of 1812 is necessary to appreciate how the United
States finally gained its true independence as a nation.

        Several important events drew the United States into
the War of 1812. These events began in Europe in 1806, when
Napoleon tried to prevent British goods from entering his
European empire. Great Britain fought back by blockading
French ports. Each country attacked any foreign ship that
tried to trade with the other country. At that time, the
United States had a booming economy and was an important
trading partner of both Great Britain and France. Both
countries attacked the American trading ships (Nardo 16).

        The United States was most angry with Great Britain,
though. One reason for this anger was that the British were
seizing American sailors and "impressing" them, or forcing
them to serve on British ships. Living conditions on the
ships were so bad that British sailors refused to serve on
them (Nardo 16). According to Gallagher, this was one of
the most important causes of America's anger with Great
Britain:

                The impressment of American sailors into the service
                of the Royal Navy [. . .] was a much larger causal
                factor of the war than often interpreted [. . .] and

The first paragraph presents the thesis statement of the report.

The first part of the report gives background about the war and is organized in time order (or chronologically) and by causes and effects.

This long quotation is indented and is not set off with quotation marks. No parenthetical citation is needed, because the author is mentioned in the preceding paragraph and the source has no page numbers. The ellipsis points (. . .) indicate where material in the source was left out.

39

it was an incredible blow to American national honor and pride. United States sovereignty was being challenged, and the American people felt that they needed to stand up to the challenge presented to them.

Americans were also outraged when Britain ruled that no neutral nation could trade with any European nation except by using British ports (Nardo 17).

President Thomas Jefferson finally decided to teach both Great Britain and France a lesson. In December 1807, he convinced Congress to pass the Embargo Act. This act stated that the United States would no longer trade with Britain or France or with any other countries that traded with them. This act actually hurt the United States and helped Britain, though, because it allowed Britain to trade with the countries that the United States no longer traded with. The attempt to weaken Britain's economy seemed only to weaken the U.S. economy and government (Morris 12).

When James Madison became president in 1809, he continued to hope that the Embargo Act would cause Great Britain to change its policy. Later that year, however, he realized that this was not going to happen, and he reopened American trade to all countries except Britain and France. The government also passed an act stating that the United States could begin trading with Britain and France once they stopped violating Americans' rights at sea (Morris 14). These actions had little effect, and the U.S. economy continued to suffer.

In addition to the trade problems with Europe, the United States had other problems. The country was expanding westward, and white settlers wanted to take over Indian

This documentation refers to source material that the write summarized.

This sentence provides a transition between the preceding paragraph and the new information that will be presented.

40

lands in the South and West. The Native Americans who lived there were allies of Britain and were a threat to the settlers (Marrin 15). Henry Clay, who was the Speaker of the House of the Twelfth Congress, was the leader of a group of congressmen known as the war hawks. They wanted war with both the Native Americans and Great Britain in order to claim the land they felt was theirs ("Causes"). They also wanted to prove to the British that they could not trample America's honor, even with the Native Americans on their side (Asimov 215).

George Washington once said, "To be prepared for war is one of the most effectual means of preserving peace" (Bartlett). The war hawks had set the stage for war, and President Madison realized that the country could not suffer economically any longer and that something had to be done. Even though the country was ill prepared, he declared war against Great Britain in the spring of 1812. The fighting began soon after.

This information comes from an unpaged on-line source.

Most of the battles of the war took place along the Canadian border, around the Chesapeake Bay, and along the coast of the Gulf of Mexico. The first U.S. campaign of the War of 1812 was directed against Canada, which was under British rule. President Madison decided to attack the important water route from the Great Lakes along the St. Lawrence River to the Atlantic Ocean. Soldiers approached Canada from three different directions, ready to fight. Yet everything imaginable went wrong. The armies were poorly trained, short of supplies, and often headed by people with little or no military experience. In addition, many U.S. soldiers refused to fight on Canadian soil (Asimov 221).

The topic sentence of the paragraph shows that this part of the report will deal with the actual battles and events of the war. This part is organized chronologically.

The British took advantage of these weaknesses and forced U.S. troops to surrender in the first battle of the

War of 1812, the Battle of Detroit. British forces also took Fort Mackinac, and Native Americans fighting for the British captured several other American forts, including Fort Dearborn (Carter 22).

The United States suffered other defeats. The worst of these was the Battle of Washington, D.C. In 1814, Great Britain had defeated Napoleon, and tens of thousands of British troops were freed to fight in North America. They entered the Chesapeake Bay in the late summer of 1814, planning to attack Washington and Baltimore. The secretary of war assured Americans that there was no danger, but the British began to move in. There were only a few U.S. troops in the area, and they were not well prepared. After a brief battle, the Americans realized that they were greatly outnumbered by the British army and ran for their lives (Nardo 82).

The British did not stop there but moved on to destroy the U.S. capital. On August 25, 1814, British troops marched into the heart of Washington, D.C., burning every government building, including the White House. As the capital of the newly founded nation burned to ashes, the British felt certain that it would not be long before the rest of the nation fell too. The United States had to prove them wrong, and it went on the offensive ("Battle"). From then on, U.S. troops began winning battles, including the Battle of Baltimore. It was during this battle that Francis Scott Key wrote the poem known as "The Star Spangled Banner," which became our national anthem.

U.S. forces were also doing well at sea. U.S. ships were very well made and were manned by courageous, well-trained officers and expert crewmen. One of these ships, the

U.S.S. <u>Constitution</u>, managed to escape a confrontation with five British ships off the coast of New Jersey. The crew of the <u>Constitution</u> and the British crews had to attach their ships to rowboats and row them for two long days and nights when the wind stopped blowing. Finally, the wind picked up again and the <u>Constitution</u> left the British ships behind (Marrin 54-55).

When a citation includes more than one page, give both page numbers in their entirety for numbers under 100.

Until the War of 1812, no British ship had ever been defeated by an enemy ship of the same class. By the end of the first six months of the war, 16 U.S. warships had captured 450 British merchant ships (Carter 25). Despite these U.S. victories during the first year of the war, the British managed in 1813 to blockade most of the eastern U.S. coast, preventing the United States from trading with other countries (Morris 8).

By 1814 the Americans and the British had won and lost similar numbers of battles. On December 24, 1814, after two and a half years of brutal fighting and thousands of deaths on both sides, the two countries signed a peace treaty in Ghent. Neither side had achieved complete victory, so neither side was forced to surrender. The agreement was that each side would release all prisoners and would return all property that belonged to the other side ("Treaty of Ghent"). President Madison stated that the peace treaty was "highly honorable to the United States" (Elting 327). In fact, though, it did not even deal with the impressment of U.S. sailors or with shipping rights, the original issues that had forced the United States into the war. Americans were ready for peace, though, and accepted the treaty. It is interesting that, because news traveled so slowly in those days, a major battle of the war, the Battle of New Orleans, was fought two weeks after the peace treaty had been signed.

This sentence introduces the conclusion of the report by asking readers to think about the meaning of the information presented.

So what did the United States gain by fighting a two-and-a-half-year war that left both countries essentially the way they were before? One answer is that it began to develop a major weapons industry. Manufacturing plants and companies grew in size and even started to sell their weapons to other countries, giving a big boost to the U.S. economy. Another answer is that the capture of land from Native Americans allowed the United States to expand westward. Although this expansion was good for the United States as a whole, it brought great suffering to the Native Americans (Elting 12).

The conclusion gives information that ties up loose ends and restates the thesis of the report.

As a result of the treaty, the United States also began to trade peacefully with Britain and to sign agreements that allowed the two countries to build a positive and lasting relationship (Nardo 104-06). In that way, both nations were winners. Americans could feel a new pride in their country as strong nation able to deal with other nations as an equal. They had fought—and won—their second war for independence.

44

Works Cited

Asimov, Isaac. The Birth of the United States, 1763-1816.
    Boston: Houghton, 1974.

"The Battle of Washington D.C." War of 1812-1814. 7 Apr.
    2000 <http://members.tripod.com/~war1812/
    batwash.html>.

Bartlett, John. Familiar Quotations. 9th ed. Boston:
    Little, 1901. 10 Apr. 2000 <http://www.bartleby.com/
    99/281.html>.

Carter, Alden R. The War of 1812: Second Fight for
    Independence. New York: Watts, 1992.

"Causes of the War." The War of 1812. 6 Apr. 2000
    <http://www2.andrews.edu/~downm/causes.html>.

Elting, John R. Amateurs, to Arms!: A Military History of
    the War of 1812. Chapel Hill: Algonquin, 1991.

Gallagher, James. "Impressment of American Seamen: The Main
    Reason for the War of 1812." Old Dominion University
    Historical Review 1.1 (1994). 7 Apr. 2000 <http://
    www.odu.edu/~hanley/history1/Gallagr2.htm>.

Marrin, Albert. 1812, the War Nobody Won. New York:
    Atheneum, 1985.

Morris, Richard B. The War of 1812. Minneapolis: Lerner,
    1985.

Nardo, Don. The War of 1812. San Diego: Lucent, 1991.

"Treaty of Ghent." War of 1812. Galafilm. 10 Apr. 2000
    <http://www.galafilm.com/1812/e/events/ghent.html>.

Think and Respond

In your learning log, in your writing folder, or in a group discussion, analyze the sample research report on the previous pages. Respond to these questions about the report:

1. What information appears in the heading of the report? at the top of each page?

2. What is the main idea, or thesis, of the report? Does the writer support her thesis? How?

3. What are the major parts of the body of the report? What is the main point in each part? Does the order of the parts make sense? Why or why not?

4. How does the writer of the report indicate, within the report, that she has taken material from a source?

5. Where does the writer's complete list of sources appear, and what is it called?

6. Does the writer use a wide variety of sources? What different kinds of sources does she use?

7. How does the writer introduce her report?

8. How does the writer conclude her report?

9. Does the writer use evidence skillfully to support the claims that she makes? Give two examples.

10. What suggestions for improvement might you give this writer?

Discovering a Topic for Research

One of the most important parts of doing a research report is choosing a topic. By choosing wisely, you can ensure that your research will go smoothly and that you will enjoy doing it.

Choosing a Subject That You Care About

A **subject** is a broad area of interest, such as African-American history or animal behavior. One way to approach the search for a research-report topic is first to choose a general area of interest and then to focus on some part of it. Make sure that you have a real reason for wanting to explore the subject. Often the best subjects for research reports are ones that are related to your own life or to the lives of people you know.

If you are already keeping a "writing ideas" list in your journal or in your writing portfolio, you can refer to that list for possible subjects. If you are not regularly listing your writing ideas, you might consider starting to do so now.

You can begin exploring general subject areas that interest you by completing the following interest inventory.

❝ Often the best subjects for research reports are ones that are related to your own life or to the lives of people you know. **❞**

Interest Inventory

Respond in writing to the following questions:

1. What subjects do I enjoy reading about?

2. What topics that I have recently read about in magazines or seen on television would I like to know more about?

Interest Inventory (cont.)

3. What books have I enjoyed reading in the past?

4. What subjects have captured my attention and interest in my classes?

5. What issues do I feel strongly about?

6. What kind of topic do I want to write about—an event, a person, or an idea?

7. What interesting careers or hobbies do my friends, acquaintances, and relatives have? What interesting experiences have they had?

8. If I could have a long conversation with someone from any place and from any time in history, who would that person be?

9. What do I wonder about? What aspects of my world would I like to know the origins or history of?

If your answers to the interest-inventory questions don't suggest a general subject area that you would like to learn more about, try the following activities.

Searching for a Subject

1. Spend some time in a library, simply walking up and down the aisles or browsing through the catalog, looking for subjects that appeal to you.

2. Browse through encyclopedias, almanacs, atlases, dictionaries, or recent periodical indexes. Useful indexes include the *Readers' Guide to Periodical Literature* and *Historical Abstracts*.

Searching for a Subject (cont.)

3. If your school or library has any books with lists of ideas for research reports, look through these.

4. Glance at the tables of contents in your textbooks, looking for subjects that you'd like to know more about.

5. If you have access to an electronic encyclopedia, a knowledge database, or a computer index that covers general subjects, start with an interesting search word and see where that leads. If you have access to the Internet, you could try browsing the World Wide Web for topics that interest you.

6. Watch public-television specials, or listen to public-radio programs. See if any of the subjects of the programs capture your imagination.

7. Look through newsmagazines for subjects related to current events.

8. List some novels that you have read or films that you have seen, and think about possible subjects related to these.

> "Spend some time in a library, simply walking up and down the aisles or browsing through the catalog, looking for subjects that appeal to you."

Limiting Your Subject/Choosing a Topic

Once you have a **general subject** that you are interested in, such as endangered species or civil rights, the next step is to narrow that subject to a **specific topic** that can be treated in a research report.

Doing Preliminary Research

If you already know a great deal about your subject, then you can probably think of a specific topic to research in that subject area. However, if you are not already an expert, it is a good idea to do some preliminary research to identify potential topics. Here are a few suggestions for preliminary research.

Ideas for Preliminary Research

- Read encyclopedia articles.

- List questions about the subject, and interview someone knowledgeable about it.

- Brainstorm with friends, classmates, or relatives to find out what they know about the subject.

- Check the *Readers' Guide to Periodical Literature* to find general articles on your subject.

- Find a textbook that covers the general field of study to which your subject belongs. Read about your subject in that textbook.

- Go to the place in the library where books on the subject are shelved. Choose books at random and look them over.

Here is how one student conducted her preliminary research.

One Student's Process: Jenny

In searching for a subject for her research report, Jenny watched a television program about wars the United States had been involved in. She knew quite a bit about the Civil War already, because her brother was really interested in it and her family had visited many battle sites on their vacations. She had also heard a lot about World War II from her grandfather and about the Vietnam War from her father and her uncles. She knew hardly anything about the War of 1812, though. She wondered what the program's description of the war as the "second war for independence" meant. She decided to find out.

Using Prewriting Techniques

In addition to conducting preliminary research, you may want to use one of the following prewriting techniques to help you come up with a specific topic:

1. **Freewriting or clustering.** Write whatever comes to mind about the subject for five minutes, or draw a cluster diagram in which you use lines to connect your subject with related ideas.

2. **Brainstorming.** Working with a group of friends or classmates, write down a list of topics that come to mind as people think about the subject.

3. **Questioning.** Write a list of questions about the subject. Begin each question with the word *who, what, where, when, why,* or *how,* or start your questions with *What if . . .*

4. **Discussing.** Listen to what other students know about your subject, what interests them about it, and what problems they think you might have in researching it.

Evaluating Possible Topics

Once you have come up with a list of ideas for possible topics, you need to evaluate them—that is, you need to judge them on the basis of certain criteria. Here are some criteria for judging a research topic:

1. **The topic should be interesting.** Often the most interesting topic is one that is related to your family's history, to your future, to your major goals, to the place where you live or would like to live, to a career that interests you, or to a hobby or other activity that you enjoy. The topic might be something that has caught your interest in the past, perhaps something you have read about or have studied in school.

2. **The topic should be covered in readily available sources.** When considering a topic, always check the catalogs of a few local libraries and the *Readers' Guide to Periodical Literature* to see if sources are available.

> "The topic might be something that has caught your interest in the past, perhaps something you have read about or have studied in school."

3. The topic should be significant. Choose a topic that is significant for you, one worth your time and energy.

4. The topic should be objective. Make sure that you will be able to gather enough facts about the topic to support your argument.

5. You should not simply repeat material available in other sources. You should look for a topic that allows you to come up with your own angle or approach.

6. The topic should be narrow enough to be treated fully. Ask your teacher how many pages long your paper should be, and choose a topic that is narrow enough to be treated in a paper of that length.

Writing a Statement of Controlling Purpose

Once you have decided on a specific topic, your next step is to write a **statement of controlling purpose.** This is a sentence or pair of sentences that tells what you want to accomplish in your report. It is called a statement of controlling purpose because it controls, or guides, your research. The statement of controlling purpose usually contains one or more keywords that tell what the report is going to accomplish. Keywords that often appear in statements of controlling purpose include *analyze, classify, compare, contrast, define, describe, determine, establish, explain, identify, prove,* and *support.*

Here are two examples of statements of controlling purpose:

The purpose of this report is to analyze the impact of the use of solar energy on pollution.

The purpose of this report is to contrast the leadership styles of President Harry S. Truman and Premier Joseph Stalin during the period 1945–1952.

To come up with a statement of controlling purpose, you will probably have to do a good deal of preliminary research. That is because before you can write a statement of controlling purpose, you need to know enough about your topic to have a general idea of what you want to say in your report. Here is an example of one student's process.

One Student's Process: Jenny

In doing her preliminary research, Jenny realized that she was interested in the big picture of the War of 1812. She decided that to paint this picture for her readers, she would need to give a broad overview of the events that led up to the war, the battles of the war itself, and the effects of the war on the United States. To do this in the small number of pages of her report, she would have to focus on the important issues rather than on small details about individual people and events.

Since she was interested in getting all the important facts about the war, she searched her library's computer catalog for the broad term *War of 1812*. She also used those words as the basis of an Internet search. As she gathered information about the war, she wrote the following statement of controlling purpose: "The purpose of this report is to explain why the War of 1812 was important in the development of the United States and why it is sometimes called the 'second war for independence.'"

Here are some examples of types of controlling purposes:

Statements of Controlling Purpose

A controlling purpose can involve . . .

Supporting (or arguing against) a policy: The purpose of this paper is to support the policy of limiting nuclear weapons.

Proving (or disproving) one or more statements of fact: The purpose of this paper is to prove that by failing to take action against Italy, the League of Nations was partly responsible for that country's takeover of Ethiopia in 1936.

> "To come up with a statement of controlling purpose, you will probably have to do a good deal of preliminary research."

Determining the relative values of two or more things: The purpose of this paper is to compare land-war tactics and air-war tactics to determine which type of warfare is more effective in a jungle war.

Analyzing something into its parts and showing how the parts relate to one another: The purpose of this paper is to describe the roles of various citizen groups and government agencies in making policies that affect support for the homeless.

Defining something: The purpose of this paper is to define the phrase *freedom of the press* by describing the laws that limit it.

Explaining causes or effects: The purpose of this paper is to explain the causes of the destruction of Brazil's rain forests.

Establishing a cause-effect relationship: The purpose of this paper is to show that increasing state and federal spending on education leads to improved test scores.

Describing the development of something over time: The purpose of this paper is to describe how rock 'n' roll developed from blues, gospel, and country music.

Identifying and describing a general trend: The purpose of this paper is to describe the extinction of South American plant and animal species that is now occurring.

Classifying items into groups or categories: The purpose of this paper is to classify African myths into categories such as creation stories and ancestor stories.

Relating a part to a whole: The purpose of this paper is to examine the Food Stamp Program as part of the federal government's welfare system in the 1970s.

Comparing or contrasting two things to show how they are similar or different: The purpose of this paper is to compare the actions of the guerrillas in the Pacific theater during World War II with the actions of the Vietcong in the Vietnam War.

Examining a technique: The purpose of this paper is to look at persuasive techniques used in television ads.

Explaining a general concept by means of specific examples: The purpose of this paper is to explain the idea of balance of power by giving examples of it in action.

Explaining the main idea or message of something: The purpose of this paper is to explain the political message of George Orwell's *1984.*

This list of types of controlling purpose is far from complete, so do not worry if the controlling purpose that you come up with does not fall into one of the categories in the list. Remember, though, that your controlling purpose should be one that has meaning for you and your readers.

Your controlling purpose may change as you do your research. When you begin writing your research report, you will replace your statement of controlling purpose with a **thesis statement,** a statement of your main idea. The thesis statement will not contain the phrase "the purpose of this report is." For more information on writing thesis statements, see pages 79–81.

Finding and Recording Your Sources

Once you have written a statement of controlling purpose, you are ready to put together a list of potential sources. This list of sources that might be useful to you in writing your paper is called a **working bibliography.** You will already have used some sources during your preliminary research, and you will probably want to include some or all of those sources in your working bibliography. As you continue to research and draft, you may discover that some of the sources in your initial list are not useful, and you might find new sources to add to the list. Before you decide to add any source to your list, however, be sure to evaluate it. Information on how to evaluate a source can be found on pages 57–58. See pages 25–31 for a discussion of primary and secondary sources.

Both print and nonprint sources will be available to you, and you will want to take advantage of both. Here are some good places to start looking for information:

1. Other people. People can be a researcher's greatest resource. Consider interviewing a professor at a local college or university or people who work for businesses, museums, historical societies, or other organizations.

2. Institutions and organizations. Museums, art galleries, state and local historical societies, and businesses are good sources of information about some topics. Many institutions and organizations have sites on the Internet.

3. The government. Many libraries have special departments that contain government publications. For some topics, you may want to contact town, city, county, state, or federal government offices directly. Listings of government departments and agencies can be found in telephone directories.

4. The library/media center. Remember that a library is more than just a place for housing books. Libraries also contain

> " People can be a researcher's greatest resource. "

periodicals—such as newspapers, magazines, and journals—and most have many nonprint materials, such as audio recordings, videotapes, computer software, reproductions of artworks, and pamphlets. Many libraries also provide access to the Internet.

5. Bookstores. For some topics, the latest information can be found at your local bookstore. If you do not find what you are looking for, ask a bookstore employee to look up your subject or author in *Books in Print.*

6. Bibliographies. A **bibliography** is a list of books and other materials about a particular topic. Your reference librarian can point you to general bibliographies dealing with many subjects, such as chemistry, the humanities, or plays by Shakespeare. You can also look for bibliographic lists in the backs of books about your topic.

7. On-line information services. An **on-line information service,** or **computer information service,** is an information source that can be communicated with by means of a personal computer and a modem. For information about on-line computer services, see Appendix A on pages 101–102.

8. Reference works. Reference works include almanacs, atlases, bibliographies, dictionaries, encyclopedias, periodical indexes, and thesauri. You will find these and similar works in the reference department of your library.

9. Other sources. Do not neglect television programs, live theater performances, radio shows, recordings, videotapes, computer software, and other possible sources of information. Many libraries have extensive collections of audiovisual materials of all kinds, on a wide variety of subjects. Make use of these.

Evaluating Possible Sources

After you locate a potential source, you need to decide whether it will be useful to you. The following questions will help you to evaluate a source:

1. Is the source authoritative? An **authoritative source** is one that can be relied upon to provide accurate infor-

Research Tip

Local and state government offices can often be useful to people who are doing historical research. For example, a county court clerk's office might be able to help you find copies of deeds, birth records, marriage records, and other documents.

mation. Consider the reputation of the publication and of the author. Are they well respected?

2. Is the source unbiased? An **unbiased source** is one whose author lacks any prejudices that might make his or her work unreliable. For example, a newsletter article claiming that there is no relationship between smoking and disease would probably be biased if written by someone who works for a tobacco company.

3. Is the source up-to-date? For some topics, such as ones associated with current events or with new technology, up-to-date sources are essential, so check the date on the copyright page of your source. For other topics, the copyright date may be less important or not important at all. If, for example, you were writing about 19th-century pioneer women in Wyoming, the old diaries and letters of such women would be excellent sources.

4. Is the work written at an appropriate level? Materials that are written for children are usually simplified and may be misleading. Other materials are so technical that they can be understood only after years of study.

5. Is the source highly recommended? One way to evaluate a source is to ask an expert or authority whether the source is reliable. You can also check the bibliography in a respected source. If a source is listed in a bibliography, then it is probably considered reliable by the author or editor who put that bibliography together.

Preparing Bibliography Cards

Every time you find a source that may be useful for your research report, you need to prepare a **bibliography card** for it. All of your bibliography cards, taken together, make up your working bibliography.

A bibliography card serves three basic purposes. First, it enables you to find the source again. Second, it enables you to prepare documentation for your paper. **Documentation** is material included in a research report to identify the sources from which information was taken. Third, it enables you to prepare the Works Cited list that will appear at the end of your report. The **Works Cited list** is a complete record of the sources referred to in the report. Here is a sample bibliography card.

Bibliography card for a book by a single author

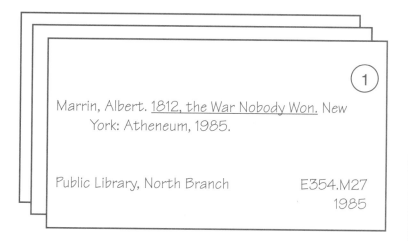

Marrin, Albert. <u>1812, the War Nobody Won.</u> New York: Atheneum, 1985.

Public Library, North Branch   E354.M27
                                              1985

①

Notice that a bibliography card contains all or most of the items described below.

1. A bibliographic entry gives essential information about a source, such as its author, its title, the place and/or date of its publication, and the pages (of a book or magazine) on which it was found. The first line of the bibliographic entry begins in the upper left-hand part of the card. Additional lines are indented a few spaces.

2. A source note tells where you found the source. The source listed on the card above was found at the North Branch of the local public library. The source note will help you find the source again if you need to do so.

3. A source number is written in the upper right-hand corner of the card and circled. Assign a different number to each source you find. You will use this number to refer to the source on note cards containing material from that source.

4. A card catalog number, if appropriate, should be included. Books and some other materials in libraries are assigned catalog numbers. If your source comes from a library and has a catalog number, you should write that number in the lower right-hand corner of the card. The catalog number will help you to find the source again.

Every time you find a possible source, follow these steps.

Evaluating and Recording Sources

1. Evaluate the source.

2. Select a blank 3″ × 5″ index card or slip of paper to use as a bibliography card.

3. Find the appropriate bibliographic form in Appendix C on pages 106–115. Then write on the card a complete bibliographic entry for the source. Make sure you capitalize and punctuate the entry properly.

4. In the top right-hand corner of the card, record a source number and circle it.

5. At the bottom of the card, record the place where you found the source.

6. If the source has a catalog number, record that number as well.

7. Stack the card with the rest of the cards that make up your working bibliography.

Research Tip

You may want to look at literary works written during a historical period you are researching. They can give you a sense of the daily life and social attitudes of that time. Other useful primary sources are journals, collections of letters, and memoirs from the period.

Gathering Information

After you have written a statement of controlling purpose and have prepared a working bibliography, you are ready to begin gathering information for your report. Begin with the most promising sources recorded on your bibliography cards—the ones that are the most general, the most authoritative, or the easiest to find. Keeping your controlling purpose clearly in mind, start searching through your sources, looking for information that applies. Do not read, view, or listen to every part of every source. Concentrate on the parts that relate to your topic and your purpose.

Some nonprint sources, such as on-line encyclopedias, have indexes or special search features that can help you to find the exact items of information that you need. If you conduct interviews as part of your research, you will be able to prepare questions beforehand so you can gather information that is directly related to your topic and purpose.

Preparing Note Cards

There are three basic types of notes:

- A **direct quotation** repeats the words of a source exactly. Quotation marks are used around the quoted material.

- A **paraphrase** states an idea expressed in a source, but not in the same words.

- A **summary** is a shortened statement of an idea in a source. In other words, it says the same thing in fewer and different words.

Take notes on 4″ × 6″ cards. Use cards of that size to distinguish your note cards from your 3″ × 5″ bibliography cards. Use a separate card for each note so that you can rearrange your notes later on. Try to limit each note to one or two sentences on

> "Do not read, view, or listen to every part of every source. Concentrate on the parts that relate to your topic and your purpose."

a single idea. Focusing on one idea on each card makes it easier to group and reorganize your cards.

When you quote, it is extremely important that you copy each letter and punctuation mark exactly. In paraphrasing or summarizing, you need to make sure that when you put the material into your own words, you do not change the source's meaning.

Give a page reference for any information taken from a source, except an entry in an encyclopedia or a dictionary:

- Information from a single page—write the page number after the note.

- Information from two or more consecutive pages—write the numbers of the first and last pages, as follows: 1–4. For consecutive numbers greater than 99, use only the last two digits of the second number, as follows: 110–15.

- Information from nonconsecutive pages in a periodical—write the number of the first page followed by a plus sign, as follows: 76+.

The following note card is well prepared. The note is brief and deals with a single idea. The four main parts of the note card have been labeled.

Source number (Take this number from the appropriate bibliography card.)

Guideline (Keep cards with similar guidelines together.)

Note (This should be a quotation, a paraphrase, a summary, or a combination of those types of notes.)

Page reference (See instructions above.)

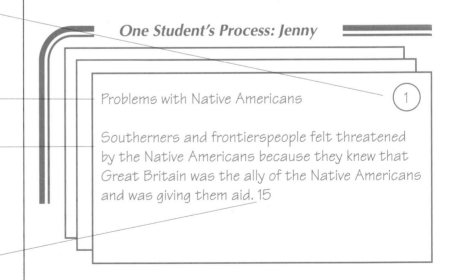

One Student's Process: Jenny

Problems with Native Americans   1

Southerners and frontierspeople felt threatened by the Native Americans because they knew that Great Britain was the ally of the Native Americans and was giving them aid. 15

The following note card needs improvement. It presents two unrelated ideas.

British trade restrictions against U.S./
Impressment

③

The British passed laws forbidding neutral nations
like the United States from trading with any
European nation except by using British ports.
These laws outraged Americans. Great Britain also
seized American sailors and forced them to serve
on British ships. 16–17

This note comes from
one section of one
source, but it contains
two different ideas.
The writer needs to
use a separate note
card for each idea.

The material on this card should be recorded on two separate cards.

When recording a direct quotation, you may wish to add a note to identify the speaker or to provide necessary background information. This short explanation can be a summary or a paraphrase. The following note card, for example, contains a summary that helps explain the quoted material.

Impressment

②

Impressment was one of the most important
causes of America's anger with Great Britain: "The
impressment of American sailors into the service
of the Royal Navy [. . .] was a much larger causal
factor of the war than often interpreted [. . .] and
it was an incredible blow to American national
honor and pride. United States sovereignty was
being challenged, and the American people felt
that they needed to stand up to the challenge presented to them."

This note begins with
a summary that
introduces a
quotation. Many of
your notes will
combine quotations
with summaries or
paraphrases.

The chart on the next page explains when to use the various types of notes.

63

When to Quote, Paraphrase, and Summarize

1. **Direct quotation.** Use a direct quotation when an idea is especially well stated in a source—that is, when a passage is very clear, beautiful, funny, or powerful. Also use a direct quotation when the exact wording is historically or legally significant or when you are reproducing a definition.

2. **Paraphrase.** Use the paraphrase as your basic note form—the form that you always use unless you have a good reason to quote or summarize your source.

3. **Summary.** Use a summary when a passage in a source is too long to be effectively quoted or paraphrased.

4. **Quotation plus summary or paraphrase.** Write this kind of note when you want to quote a source but need to give more explanation to make the quotation clear.

The following guidelines will help you to improve your note-taking skills:

Effective Note Taking

1. Keep your topic, controlling purpose, and audience in mind at all times. Do not record material unrelated to your topic.

2. Make sure that summaries and paraphrases accurately express the ideas in your sources.

Effective Note Taking (cont.)

3. Be accurate. Make sure to copy direct quotations word for word, with capitalization, spelling, and punctuation precisely as in the original. Make sure that every direct quotation begins and ends with quotation marks.

4. Double-check statistics and facts to make sure that you have them right.

5. Distinguish between fact and opinion by labeling opinions as such: "Dr. Graves thinks that . . ." or "According to Grace Jackson . . ."

6. Quote only the important parts of a passage. Indicate words you have left out by using **points of ellipsis**— a series of three spaced dots (. . .)—enclosed in brackets. Use only the three dots when cutting material within a sentence. Use a period before the dots when cutting a full sentence, a paragraph, or more than a paragraph. Use a period after the dots when you cut material from the end of a sentence. Also use brackets ([ ]) to enclose any explanatory information that you add within a quotation.

7. Always double-check page references. It's easy to copy these incorrectly.

Research Tip

When dealing with facts and statistics,
1. Use sources that are well respected and authoritative.
2. Try to check the facts and statistics in at least two different sources.
3. Always double-check the facts and statistics to make sure you are copying them accurately.

Avoiding Plagiarism

One of the purposes of your working bibliography and note cards is to help you to avoid plagiarism. **Plagiarism** is the act of intentionally or unintentionally presenting work done by someone else as though it were your own. In most schools, including middle schools, high schools, and universities, plagiarism is considered a serious offense and can result in severe penalties, such as failing grades, loss of course credit, or even expulsion.

Because plagiarism is so serious, it is important to know exactly what it is and what you can do to avoid it. Here is a simple test to determine whether something is plagiarized: ask yourself, Is this information, idea, or statement common knowledge? If the answer is no, then ask yourself, Did this information, idea, or statement come from a source outside myself, or did it come from my own experience or ideas? If the information, idea, or statement is not common knowledge, and if it came from an outside source, then you must credit that source. Failure to do so is plagiarism.

Developing a Preliminary Outline

At some point early in your research, you will come to know enough about your topic to begin to develop a **preliminary,** or rough, **outline.** A preliminary outline is useful because it will help you to focus your search for information. Your preliminary outline should list some key ideas or subtopics that you expect to include in the body of your report. As you learn more about your topic, your preliminary outline will change and grow, but even a short, incomplete preliminary outline can be useful.

One Student's Process: Jenny

Soon after Jenny began her research on the War of 1812, she decided that she would divide her report into three parts. Rather than writing a complete outline, she created this preliminary one:

Causes of the war
—trade conflicts with Europe
—impressment
—problems with Native Americans
Battles and events of the war
—British victories
—U.S. victories
—peace treaty
Results of the war
—national pride and independence
—positive trade relationship with Britain

A preliminary outline can consist of just a few entries or of many. In a preliminary outline, main entries are usually begun at the left-hand margin, and subentries are introduced by dashes.

The Note-Taking/Outlining Cycle

Writing is a cyclical process. At any point in the process, you can stop what you are doing and return to an earlier point. For example, you might decide after doing a little research to return to the very beginning and to choose a new topic, or you might decide to change your statement of controlling purpose. In other words, you are free to return to the beginning and to start the writing cycle all over again.

Nowhere in the process of preparing a research report is the cyclical nature of writing more obvious than in the gathering of information. During this stage, you will continually go back and forth between your preliminary outline and your note cards. As you do research and take notes, you will acquire more and more information that you can use to improve your outline. As you change the headings in your outline, you will want to reorganize your note cards, to change the guidelines on the note cards, and to take new notes related to your outline's headings. Your notes and your outline will grow and change together—each feeding into the other.

"Your notes and your outline will grow and change together—each feeding into the other."

67

Organizing Your Material

5

I n the preceding chapter you learned that writing a research report is a cyclical process. The more research you do, and the more information you gather on note cards, the more you will understand your topic. The more you understand your topic, the more detailed you can make your preliminary outline. The more detailed your preliminary outline becomes, the more you will understand what additional information you need to gather.

At first your preliminary outline will probably not be very detailed. To develop a detailed outline, you will need to consider, over and over again, how best to organize the information that you are gathering. Of course, as you write and research, the organization can and probably will change.

> "There are even more possible ways to organize research reports than there are possible topics."

Organizing Ideas in a Research Report

Much of the writing that people do is fiction, how-to writing, or personal correspondence, and almost all of this writing is organized chronologically. Other writing, including a great deal of nonfiction, is usually organized in what might be called **part-by-part order.** One idea or group of ideas suggests another, which suggests another, and so on to the end. Each idea is related in some way to the one that precedes it and to the one that follows it, but no single, overall method of organization is used.

There are even more possible ways to organize research reports than there are possible topics. For this reason, there are no hard-and-fast rules about how ideas in research reports should be organized. However, here are some guidelines to keep in mind:

1. Your report will begin with an introduction that states your thesis. It will end with a conclusion that restates your thesis and summarizes the main point or points of the report. You need to concentrate on organizing the body of the report. Your goal is to find a sensible method of arranging the information that you will present in the body.

2. Many topics require that you start by providing background information. If you have chosen such a topic, think about what background information should appear early on, and group that information together. Among this background information, you might want to include definitions of any key terms that will appear in your paper.

3. Remember that events are usually presented in chronological order unless there is a good reason to present them in some other way. So if part or all of your paper involves presenting events, consider organizing those events chronologically.

4. As you gather your notes, or evidence, sort the note cards into separate piles of related ideas and information. Try different combinations, and make rough outlines based on them.

5. Once you have your note cards separated into piles of related ideas and information, come up with a phrase to describe what is in each pile. Think about the different orders in which you could present each group of ideas. Ask yourself, Should the ideas in pile one be presented first, or those in pile three? Why?

6. Look for relationships among the ideas in each group of note cards. Also look for relationships among groups of cards. The following chart describes some of the relationships that you might discover and build on.

Ways to Relate Ideas

1. **Chronological order:** from first event to last event or from last event to first event

2. **Spatial order:** by arrangement in space

3. **Classification:** in groups sharing similar properties or characteristics

Ways to Relate Ideas (cont.)

4. **Order of degree:** according to importance, value, interest, obviousness, certainty, or a similar quality

5. **Cause-and-effect order:** from cause to effect or from effect to cause

6. **Comparison-and-contrast order:** from similarities to differences or from differences to similarities

7. **Analytical order:** according to parts and relationships among the parts

8. **Inductive order, or synthesis:** from specific examples to generalizations based on those examples

9. **Deductive order:** from a general idea or principle to specific conclusions based on that general idea or principle

10. **Order of impression, or association:** according to the sequence in which things strike one's attention

11. **Hierarchical order:** from class to subclass (group within a class) or from subclass to class

Creating a Draft Outline

Before beginning your rough draft, you will want to create a draft outline. A **draft outline** is a formal outline that is used as a basis for a rough draft. It can be a **sentence outline,** containing entries that are all complete sentences, or it can be a **topic outline,** containing entries that are words, phrases, or clauses.

A draft outline begins with a statement of controlling purpose. It is divided into two or more major sections introduced by Roman numerals (I, II). Each major section is divided into two or more subsections introduced by capital letters (A, B). The subsections may be divided into sub-subsections introduced by Arabic numerals (1, 2), and those into sub-sub-subsections introduced by lowercase letters (a, b).

One Student's Process: Jenny

Jenny wrote a draft outline for her report on the War of 1812. She decided to write a topic outline.

Topic Outline

```
        The Second War for Independence
Controlling Purpose: The purpose of this
report is to discuss the causes of the War
of 1812, the battles and other events that
took place, and the effects of the war on
the development of the United States. This
information will explain why the war is
known as the second war for independence.
   I.  Causes of the War of 1812
       A. Trade conflicts with Great Britain
          and France
       B. Impressment of U.S. sailors by
          Britain
       C. Responses by the U.S. government
          1. Embargo Act
          2. Failure of the act
       D. Problems with Native Americans
          1. Alliance with Great Britain
          2. Responses by war hawks
  II.  Battles and events of the war
       A. British victories
          1. Battle of Detroit
          2. Fort Mackinac and Fort Dearborn
          3. Battle of Washington
       B. U.S. victories
          1. Battle of Baltimore
          2. U.S.S. Constitution
       C. Peace treaty
          1. No clear winner and no surrender
```

When preparing a formal outline for submission to a teacher or to a peer reviewer, always double-space the outline. On the first page of the outline, include your name, your teacher's name, the name of your class, and the date, as shown in the sample research report on page 39 of this book. If there are additional pages, include your last name and the page number in the upper right-hand corner of each.

2. Release of prisoners and return
   of property
III. Results of the war
   A. Growth at home
      1. Weapons industry
      2. Westward expansion
   B. New international position
      1. Positive trade relationship with
         Britain
      2. Equal of other countries
   C. Independence as a nation

You might want to add a conclusion at the end of your outline, stating the main point you want to make in your research report.

Here is how the first section of the outline would look as a sentence outline:

I. Several international and domestic
   events combined to cause the War of
   1812.
   A. As a result of trade conflicts
      between Great Britain and France,
      each country began attacking U.S.
      ships that tried to trade with the
      other.
   B. Great Britain angered the United
      States by impressing its sailors,
      or seizing them and making them
      serve in its navy.
   C. The U.S. government responded to
      these actions by trying to make
      Great Britain and France suffer
      economically.
      1. Congress passed the Embargo Act,
         which prohibited U.S. trade with
         Britain, France, and any nation
         that traded with them.
      2. The act was not effective because
         instead of harming Britain's
         trade and economy, it actually
         improved them.

Drafting Your Research Report

A fter completing a draft outline and arranging your note cards to match the outline, you are ready to begin writing your rough draft. The comforting thing about a rough draft is that it does not have to be perfect. You can rework your draft as often as you like and watch it take shape gradually. In other words, you do not have to hit a home run your first time at bat. You can have as many chances at the plate as you want.

Approaches to Drafting

With regard to drafting, writers fall into two major camps. Some prefer to get everything down on paper quickly, but in very rough form, and then do one or more detailed revisions. Others like to complete each section as they go, writing and polishing one section, then moving on to the next. Either approach is fine. If you choose the second approach, however, you might want to look first at pages 82–86, which give information about revision.

The Style of the Draft

A research report is a type of objective, formal writing. Therefore, you should avoid making the paper personal and subjective, and you should avoid using informal language. Do not use such words as *I, me, my, mine, we,* and *our.* Do not state opinions without supporting them with facts. Do not use slang, informal language, or contractions.

Assembling the Draft

A rough draft is just that—it is rough, or unfinished. As you draft, do not worry about matters that you can take care of later,

> " You do not have to hit a home run your first time at bat. You can have as many chances at the plate as you want. "

such as details of spelling, grammar, usage, and mechanics. Instead, concentrate on getting your ideas down in an order that makes sense.

Use your outline as a guide. Explore each main point, supporting the idea with evidence from your note cards. When you use information from a note card in your draft, include the source number from the note card and circle it. Noting the source number is extremely important because during revision you will have to find the source in order to document it.

━━ **One Student's Process: Jenny** ━━

Here is one of the entries in Jenny's outline for her report on the War of 1812:

```
Problems with Native Americans
```

Jenny turned this phrase into a statement, which she used as the topic sentence for a paragraph in her report

```
In addition to the trade problems
with Europe, the United States had other
problems.
```

Then she added material from her note cards to support the topic sentence:

```
        The country was expanding westward,
and white settlers wanted to take over
Indian lands in the South and West. The
Native Americans who lived there were
allies of Britain and were a threat to
the settlers. (1) Henry Clay, who was the
Speaker of the House of the Twelfth
Congress, was the leader of a group of
congressmen known as the war hawks. They
wanted war with both the Native Americans
and Great Britain in order to claim the
land they felt was theirs. (8)
```

Notice that Jenny added paraphrased material to support the topic sentence. She included source numbers from note cards so that she would be able to find information about these sources later on, when she was preparing the documentation, or full source information, for her report.

Incorporating summaries and paraphrases. Working summaries and paraphrases into your report is quite easy. Simply write them out as part of your text and include a source number at the end of the summarized or paraphrased material. Just be certain to use transitions to connect the material smoothly to the sentences that precede or follow it.

Incorporating quotations. Working quotations into your paper is a bit more complicated because there are many ways in which quotations can be used. Also, the rules for prose differ from those for poetry or song lyrics. See the chart on pages 76–77 for complete instructions on using quotations in your draft.

The Draft as a Work in Progress

As you write, you may occasionally discover gaps in the information that you have gathered. In other words, you may find that you do not have in your note cards all the information you need to make some point. When this occurs, you can stop and look for the information, or you can simply make a note to yourself to find the information later on. Either approach works well.

The need to fill gaps is one proof that drafting is still discovery time. In addition to discovering gaps to be filled, you may discover better ways to organize parts of the report, ideas in your source materials that conflict, or parts of your topic that you have not yet explored. You may even find a whole new approach to your topic, one more interesting or workable than the one you have taken. Remain open to the discoveries that occur as you draft. Be willing to return, if necessary, to earlier stages of the writing process to do more research, to rethink your controlling purpose, or to change your outline.

> " Drafting is still discovery time. "

Quoting Prose Works

1. If a quotation is four lines long or less, put it in quotation marks and place it in the text of your report:

   ```
   George Washington once said, "To be prepared for war
   is one of the most effectual means of preserving
   peace."(4)
   ```

   The circled number is the source number from your note card. When you do your final documentation, you will replace this number with a citation in parentheses. (See pages 87–92.)

2. You do not have to quote complete sentences:

   ```
   President Madison stated that the peace treaty was
   "highly honorable to the United States."(6)
   ```

3. You can also break a quotation into two parts:

   ```
   "The impressment of American sailors into the service
   of the Royal Navy," according to Gallagher, "was a
   much larger causal factor of the war than often inter-
   preted."(2)
   ```

4. When a quoted passage is more than four lines long, set it off from the text of your report. Put a colon after the statement that introduces the quotation. Begin a new line. Indent the entire quotation ten spaces from the left-hand margin. Double-space the quotation, and do not enclose it in quotation marks:

   ```
   According to Gallagher, this was one of the most
   important causes of America's anger with Great Britain:

        The impressment of American sailors into the ser-
        vice of the Royal Navy [. . .] was a much larger
        causal factor of the war than often interpreted
        [. . .] and it was an incredible blow to American
        national honor and pride. United States sovereignty
        was being challenged, and the American people felt
        that they needed to stand up to the challenge pre-
        sented to them.(2)
   ```

5. When quoting more than one paragraph, indent the first line of each full paragraph an additional three spaces. However, indent the first sentence only if it begins a paragraph in your source:

Quoting Prose Works (cont.)

Impressment had been going on for many years. It was beginning to look as if Americans had had enough:

> The debates and complaints about impressment grew until the United States could no longer accept the punches to its pride. The nation went on a path towards war.
>
> The United States government rarely objected to Great Britain seizing British deserters in British ports. The United States never denied the British claims of entitlement to its own seamen. Harsh disagreement, however, stood between the two nations when it came to the subject of taking persons from American vessels on the high seas or in American waters. In the eyes of the United States government, this violated upstanding principles of international law. (2)

Quoting Poetry, Verse Plays, and Songs

1. When quoting a single line or part of a line, simply place the material in your text with quotation marks around it:

   Shakespeare's Macbeth says, "Life's but a walking shadow." (4)

2. When quoting two or three lines, separate the lines with a space, a slash (/), and another space:

   Shakespeare's Macbeth says: "Life's but a walking shadow, a poor player / That struts and frets his hour upon the stage,/ And then is heard no more." (4)

3. When quoting four or more lines, set the material off from your text. Indent it ten spaces, double-space it, and do not enclose it in quotation marks. Follow the line division and spacing of the original.

   Shakespeare's Macbeth says:

   > Life's but a walking shadow, a poor player,
   > That struts and frets his hour upon the stage
   > And then is heard no more. It is a tale
   > Told by an idiot, full of sound and fury,
   > Signifying nothing. (4)

Using Graphic Aids

As you draft, think about using tables, maps, charts, diagrams, and other **graphic aids** to present a lot of information in a little space. If you use a graphic aid from a source, or if you use information from a source to create a graphic aid, then you must credit the source of the information.

Tables should be labeled "Table 1," "Table 2," and so on. Other graphic aids should be labeled "Fig. 1," "Fig. 2," and so on. Place the label after the figure and follow it with a caption that is either the title or a description of the graphic aid. Follow that with a source credit in endnote form (see pages 116–126).

One Student's Process: Jenny

While doing her research, Jenny found a map that helped her understand what the United States was like at the time of the War of 1812. She created a graphic based on that map to go along with her report.

Fig. 1. The United States in 1812. Adapted from Miriam Greenblatt, America at War: The War of 1812 (New York: Facts on File, 1994) 39.

Writing the Introduction

The introduction of a research report should accomplish two purposes:

1. It should grab readers' attention.

2. It should present the report's main idea, or **thesis statement.**

In addition, the introduction may define key terms, supply necessary background information, or both. The introduction can be of any length, although most introductions are one or two paragraphs long.

Capturing Your Readers' Attention

There are many ways to capture readers' attention in an introduction. You can begin with an unusual fact, with a question, with an anecdote (a brief story that makes a point), with an analogy (a comparison between the topic and something with which readers are already familiar), with a paragraph that compares or contrasts, or with examples.

Writing the Thesis Statement

To create your thesis statement, you can simply rewrite your statement of controlling purpose. Be sure to include any changes you have made in your topic during research. However, avoid using the phrase "the purpose of this report" in your final thesis statement. Notice how that phrase is eliminated in the following example:

```
Controlling Purpose: The purpose of this
report is to discuss the causes of the War
of 1812, the battles and other events that
took place, and the effects of the war on
the development of the United States. This
information will explain why the war is
known as the second war for independence.
```

> **"**The introduction of a research report should . . . grab your readers' attention [and] . . . present the report's main idea, or thesis statement.**"**

Thesis Statement: An understanding of the causes, the events, and the effects of the War of 1812 is necessary to appreciate how the United States finally gained its true independence as a nation.

For your readers to understand your thesis statement, you may have to provide some background information. In the introduction all you need to include is enough information to help them understand the thesis. You can provide additional information in the body of your report.

One Student's Process: Michael

Michael was doing a report on the history of the Bill of Rights. His thesis statement was "Although many people take the freedoms guaranteed by the Bill of Rights for granted today, they were a daring experiment in government when they were written." Because some of his readers might not be familiar with the Bill of Rights, Michael decided to explain what it is in his introduction. (His completed report is on pages 129–135.)

We, the people of the United States, enjoy freedoms that no other people in the history of the world have experienced. These freedoms are guaranteed in the first ten amendments to the U.S. Constitution, called the Bill of Rights. Today it is easy for us to take these rights for granted, but they were originally a daring experiment in a new kind of government.

In the introduction to her report, Jenny wanted to accomplish two purposes: she wanted to tell what country the United States fought against in the War of 1812, and she wanted to state her thesis, or main idea.

```
America had struggled through the
Revolutionary War and finally won its inde-
pendence from Great Britain in 1776. The
fight for independence was not over, though.
On June 18, 1812, the United States again
declared war on Great Britain. Understanding
the causes and the effects of the War of
1812 is necessary to appreciate how the
United States finally gained its true inde-
pendence as a nation.
```

Writing the Conclusion

Like an introduction, a conclusion is usually one or two paragraphs long. The most common way to conclude a research report is to restate the main idea and your main arguments in support of that idea. In addition, you may wish to use the conclusion to tie up any loose ends left in the body of your paper, to explain what accepting your thesis statement might mean, to ask readers to take some action, to explain the importance or value of what they have learned from the report, or to make predictions about the future. The conclusion is an opportunity to be imaginative. Almost anything is acceptable as long as it leaves readers satisfied that you have covered the subject well. (See the sample conclusions on pages 44 and 133 of this book.)

> **"**The conclusion is an opportunity to be imaginative. Almost anything is acceptable as long as it leaves readers satisfied that you have covered the subject well. **"**

Revising Your Research Report

After you finish drafting your research report, put it aside for a day or so. Getting some distance from the report will help you to revise it.

Expect the revision of your report to take several days, and expect to revise it more than once. One excellent approach is to do separate revisions for content and organization, for style, and for documentation. During revision, do not worry about details of spelling, grammar, usage, and mechanics. You can clean up problems in those areas later on, during the proofreading stage. All you have to do about documentation at this point is be sure to list a source number in your manuscript every place you have used a source. The next chapter will explain how to turn the source numbers into complete, final documentation.

Peer Response

At some point during the drafting process, give your report to one of your peers, or fellow students, for review. By having a peer review your report, you can find out whether you have achieved your purpose, whether you have been completely clear, and whether there are parts that cause problems for readers.

Do not worry about losing control of your work. You have the right to accept or reject any suggestions that your peer reviewer makes. Here are some questions you can ask your peer reviewer to help you get useful responses from him or her.

Questions for Peer Readers

- What do you think my main point, or thesis, is? Do you think I have proved that point? Why or why not? What could I do to make the proof stronger?

- Which sections of my report did you find most interesting or informative?

- Were any parts of my report unclear to you? Which ones and why?

- What questions do you have about my topic now that you have read my report?

Self-Evaluation

A peer reviewer's comments can give you important insights into how to improve your report. However, it is also important that you evaluate your report yourself. Ask yourself the questions on the following checklist.

Revision Checklist

CONTENT AND ORGANIZATION

General

☐ **1.** Does my report support or prove my thesis statement?

☐ **2.** Does my report have a clear introduction, body, and conclusion?

☐ **3.** Does every idea follow logically from the one before it?

☐ **4.** Have I used transitions to show connections between ideas?

Introduction

☐ **5.** Will the introduction capture my readers' attention?

☐ **6.** Does the introduction present my thesis statement clearly?

Body

☐ **7.** Does the body of my report present evidence from a variety of reliable sources?

☐ **8.** Is information from my sources presented in a combination of summary, paraphrase, and quotation?

9. Are there any gaps in my argument that I need to fill by doing additional research? Are there any points that need more support?

10. Have I deleted all unnecessary material from my report?

11. Have I cited sources for opinions presented in the report?

Conclusion

12. Did I restate my thesis in the conclusion of my report?

13. Does the conclusion summarize the main points that I have presented to support my thesis?

14. Does the conclusion give my readers a sense of completion? (Are all the loose ends tied up? Have all the parts of the thesis been supported? Have all of readers' most likely questions about the topic been addressed?)

STYLE

15. Have I varied my writing by using many kinds of sentences—short and long sentences; simple, compound, complex, and compound-complex sentences; declarative, exclamatory, and interrogative sentences; and sentences that begin with different parts of speech?

16. Have I avoided wordiness? Have I deleted unnecessary words, phrases, and clauses?

17. Have I used clear, concrete examples? Have I defined key terms?

18. Have I avoided informal language, slang, and technical words that I have not defined? Have I avoided contractions, personal references, and first-person pronouns such as *I, we, me,* and *our?*

19. Are my sentences graceful, not awkward?

DOCUMENTATION

☐ **20.** Have I avoided plagiarism by completely document-ing all materials taken from sources? Does every summary, paraphrase, or quotation have a corre-sponding source number?

☐ **21.** Is each of my direct quotations set off with quotation marks or by indention? Is each quotation accurate? Have I used it to express the idea the author of the source intended?

☐ **22.** Is there a complete bibliography card, in proper form, for every source number in the final version of my manuscript? (For information on proper biblio-graphic form, see pages 106–115.)

One Student's Process: Jenny

Jenny wrote a rough draft of her report on the War of 1812. Then she did three separate revisions of her draft: one for content and organization, another for style, and the third for documentation. She revised her content and organization by adding information that explained how the Embargo Act helped Great Britain. She also moved a sentence that was out of order. To improve the style of her report, she joined two sentences to fix a sentence frag-ment; joined two related sentences; replaced a vague and informal word, *okayed*, with a more appropriate one; and added an adverb, *actually*, to contrast the true effects of the act with the ones people had hoped for. Her changes are shown in the draft on the next page. (Compare this revised paragraph with Jenny's final version on page 40.)

President Thomas Jefferson finally decided to teach both Great Britain and France a lesson. ~~Jefferson's attempt to weaken Britain's economy seemed only to weaken the U.S. economy and government.~~ In December 1807, he convinced Congress to pass the Embargo Act. This act stated that the United States would no longer trade with Britain or France or with any other countries that traded with them. This act *actually* hurt the United States and helped Britain, though, because it allowed Britain to trade with the countries that the United States no longer traded with.

When James Madison became president in 1809, he continued to hope that the Embargo Act would cause Great Britain to change its policy. Later that year, however, he realized that was not going to happen, and he ~~okayed~~ *reopened* American trade to all countries except Britain and France. The government also passed an act, stating that the United States could begin trading with Britain and France once they stopped violating Americans' rights at sea. ⑦ These actions had little effect. *and* America's economy continued to suffer.

Preparing a Final Outline

Your teacher may ask you to submit a final outline along with the final draft of your report. If so, revise the last version of your draft outline, being sure to follow the guidelines for outlining given on pages 70–72. In most cases, either a topic outline or a sentence outline is acceptable, though your teacher may prefer one type of outline over the other. The final outline should be typed or prepared on a word processor. For information on proper manuscript form for the outline and for the rest of the paper, see pages 98–99 of this book.

Documenting Your Sources

8

Each time you use information from your note cards, write down a source number. After you revise your draft, use the source numbers in the revised draft to prepare your documentation. **Documentation** is the information in the report that tells what sources you used.

Parenthetical Documentation

The method of documentation most widely used today is called **parenthetical documentation.** (For information on endnotes, footnotes, and other methods of documentation, see Appendix D on pages 116–128.)

To use parenthetical documentation, enclose a brief reference in parentheses. The reference, which is called a **parenthetical citation,** usually consists of an author's name and a page number:

```
The government also passed an act stating that

the United States could begin trading with

Britain and France once they stopped violating

Americans' rights at sea (Morris 14).
```

The process of placing the citation in your report is called **citing a source.**

A parenthetical citation contains just enough information to help readers locate the source in the Works Cited list at the end of your report. The Works Cited list consists of bibliographic entries like those shown in Appendix C on pages 106–115.

Take a moment to look at the sample research report on pages 39–44. Study the parenthetical citations. Then look at the Works Cited list on page 45, at the end of the sample report.

Preparing Parenthetical Citations

Using parenthetical citations to document your sources helps your readers identify them easily. The following guidelines will help you to cite your sources properly:

1. Basic citation. Place the citation at the end of the sentence containing the material you are documenting. The citation should appear after the last word of the sentence but before the end mark:

> The Native Americans who lived in the West and
> South were allies of Britain and a threat to
> the settlers (Marrin 15).

2. Basic citation with author's name in text. If the name of the author is stated in the sentence, then give only the page number:

> According to Nardo, Americans were also
> outraged when Britain ruled that no neutral
> nation could trade with any European nation
> except by using British ports (17).

3. Citation of a long quotation. When documenting a long quotation that is set off from the text, place the citation after the end punctuation:

> Historians agree that impressment was one
> of the most important causes of America's anger
> with Great Britain:
>
> > The impressment of American sailors
> > into the service of the Royal Navy
> > [. . .] was a much larger causal
> > factor of the war than often
> > interpreted [. . .] and it was an
> > incredible blow to American
> > national honor and pride. United

```
States sovereignty was being chal-
lenged, and the American people
felt that they needed to stand up
to the challenge presented to them.
(Gallagher)
```

4. Citation of multiple works by one author. If the Works Cited list contains more than one work by an author, then include a shortened version of the title—usually one to four words. When shortening a title, drop any first words like *a, an,* or *the* and begin with the word that the full title is alphabetized by. So, for example, the title *Amateurs, to Arms!: A Military History of the War of 1812* might become *Amateurs.*

```
President Madison stated that the peace treaty
was "highly honorable to the United States"
(Elting, Amateurs 327).
```

5. Citation with author's name and title in text. If the name of the author and the title of the work both appear in the text of your report, use only the page number, even if more than one work by the author is listed in your Works Cited list:

```
In his book entitled 1812, the War Nobody Won,
Marrin states that the Native Americans who
lived in the West and South were allies of
Britain and were a threat to the settlers (15).
```

6. Citation of a work available in various editions. When citing a literary work available in several editions, include information that will allow readers to find the quotation in any edition. For a novel, include a chapter number:

```
Even though the War of 1812 has been described
as a small-scale conflict, it was still an out-
break of what Stephen Crane called the "red
sickness of battle" (134; ch. 24).
```

For a short story or essay, include a paragraph number: ("Meditation 17" 300; par. 7). For a play divided into acts and scenes, give the act number and the scene number, separated by a period. Omit the page number(s). If the play is printed with line numbering, include line numbers as well: (<u>Macbeth</u> 5.5. 24–28).

7. Citation of an anonymous work. When citing an anonymous work (one for which no author is identified), give the title or a shortened version of the title, followed by the page number if appropriate. Make sure that the first word in a shortened version of a title is the word by which the work is alphabetized in the Works Cited list:

```
The agreement was that each side would release

all prisoners and would return all property

that belonged to the other side ("Treaty").
```

8. Citation of an encyclopedia or a similar reference work. When citing an article in a reference work that is arranged alphabetically—an encyclopedia or a biographical dictionary, for example—give only the title or a shortened version of the title:

```
There was no winner in the War of 1812. "It

did, however, push back the Indian frontier,

increase the breach between the United States

and the British North American colonies, and

confirm the U.S.-Canadian boundary" ("History of

Canada").
```

9. Citation of a work by two or three authors. When citing a work by two or three authors, give the authors' last names and the page number:

```
The only people who suffered from the embargo

were the Americans (McKay and Berg 84).
```

10. Citation of a work by more than three authors. When citing a work by more than three authors, give the last name of the first author, followed by *et al.* and the page number if appropriate. *Et al.* is an abbreviation of Latin *et alii* or *et aliae*, meaning "and others":

```
The Battle of New Orleans, which didn't take
place until two weeks after the peace treaty
was signed, left over 700 dead and 1,400
wounded (Luders et al.).
```

11. Citation of a quotation appearing in a source. When citing a statement that is quoted by your source, use the abbreviation *qtd. in:*

```
The British approach to the peace talks was
simple and direct: "Our demands may be couched
in a single word--Submission!" (qtd. in
Greenblatt 110).
```

12. Citation of a source without page numbers. For a source without page numbers—an interview, a piece of computer software, or a recording, for example—give the name of the author or interviewee. If there is no name, give the title or a shortened version of the title:

```
The United States had to prove them wrong, and
it went on the offensive ("Battle").
```

13. Citation of a multivolume work. To cite a page number in a multivolume work that is *not* an alphabetically organized reference work, give the author's name, the volume number, a colon, and the page reference.

```
The War of 1812 was not a large-scale conflict.
The battles involved only a few thousand men,
and the total U.S. casualties were about 5,000,
"fewer than fell in an hour at Gettysburg"
(Coit 3: 108).
```

14. Citation of more than one page. When citing more than one page, use a hyphen to separate the numbers unless the pages do not directly follow each other:

```
As a result of the treaty, the United States
also began to trade peacefully with Britain and
to sign agreements that allowed the two coun-
tries to build a positive and lasting
relationship (Nardo 104-06).
```

When citing consecutive pages, give the complete form of the second number for numbers through 99: 1–2, 13–15, 35–36, 67–69. When citing larger numbers, give only the last two digits of the second number unless more digits are required to avoid confusion: 99–102, 117–18, 223–24, 1201–02, 1201–303.

Preparing the List of Works Cited

Each time you cite a source in your report, pull the bibliography card for that source from your working bibliography and place it in a new stack of Works Cited cards. When you have completed your final draft, you will have a complete set of Works Cited cards. Arrange those cards in alphabetical order. Then type up your final Works Cited list from the cards, following their style exactly. Your final Works Cited list should include a complete entry for each source that you have cited in your report. Here is a sample Works Cited list for a research report on protecting the earth's forests.

```
                                    Pappas 23

                    Works Cited

Caldicott, Helen. If You Love This Planet:

    A Plan to Heal the Earth. New York:

    Norton, 1992.
```

Czapski, Silvia. "Grassroots
     Environmentalism in Brazil."
     <u>Conservationist</u> July-Aug. 1991: 42-47.
Dietrich, William. <u>The Final Forest: The
     Battle for the Last Great Trees of the
     Pacific Northwest</u>. New York: Simon, 1992.
Frome, Michael. <u>Regreening the National
     Parks</u>. Tucson: U of Arizona P, 1992.
Hamilton, Harriet. "From Stones and Clay
     an Abundance of Trees."
     <u>Conservationist</u> Sep.-Oct. 1991: 32-35.
Harrison, Robert Pogue. <u>Forests: The
     Shadow of Civilization</u>. Chicago: U of
     Chicago P, 1992.
Kahak, E. "Perceiving the Good." <u>The
     Wilderness Condition: Essays on
     Environment and Civilization</u>. Ed. Max
     Oelschaeger. San Francisco: Sierra
     Club, 1992. 173-87.
Kernan, Henry S. "The World Is My Woodlot
     Too." <u>Conservationist</u> Jan.-Feb. 1992:
     44-47.
Ketchledge, Edwin H. "Born-Again Forest."
     <u>Natural History</u> May 1992: 34-38.
Snyder, Gary. "Etiquette of Freedom." <u>The
     Wilderness Condition: Essays on
     Environment and Civilization</u>. Ed. Max
     Oelschaeger. San Francisco: Sierra
     Club, 1992. 21-39.

"Your final Works Cited list should include a complete entry for each source that you have cited in your report."

If you use more than one work by the same author, alphabetize the works by their titles. Give the author's name for the first work. For the following works, use three hyphens in place of the name.

```
Steinbeck, John. The Grapes of Wrath.
     1939. New York: Penguin, 1976.
---. Their Blood Is Strong. San Francisco:
     Lubin, 1938. Rpt. in French, Companion
     53-92.
```

If you use several pieces from a collection of a single author's works, you can give an entry for the entire work, without listing the individual essays or articles.

Manuscript Form for the List of Works Cited

1. Begin on a new page.

2. Use one-inch margins on both sides.

3. Include your last name and the page number, flush right, half an inch from the top of the paper.

4. Drop down another one-half inch and center the title "Works Cited." Do not underline it or use all capital letters.

5. Double-space between entries. Double-space between the title and the first entry.

6. Begin each entry at the left margin. Double-space within each entry. Indent run-over lines five spaces from the left margin.

7. If you wish, you can break down your Works Cited list into categories such as "Books," "Periodicals," and so on. If you do this, list the materials under each heading alphabetically.

9

Completing Your Research Report

After you have finished your documentation, you are ready to proofread your report and to prepare your final manuscript. **Proofreading** is the process of checking your work for errors in spelling, grammar, usage, level of language, capitalization, punctuation, and documentation. The **final manuscript** is the copy of your report that will be read by your teacher and by others.

Proofreading Your Report

The first step after revising your report and preparing your documentation is proofreading it to eliminate errors. When you proofread, use symbols like those shown on page 100. Keep the following guidelines in mind when you proofread a research report.

Proofreading a Research Report

1. Double-check the spellings of proper names, such as the names of people and places.

2. Check to see that the quotations you have used fit grammatically into the sentences in which they appear.

   Ungrammatical: The War of 1812 actually "push back the Indian frontier, increase the breach between the United States and the British North American colonies, and confirm the U.S.-Canadian boundary."

   Grammatical: The War of 1812 actually did "push back the Indian frontier, increase the breach between the United

```
States and the British North American
colonies, and confirm the U.S.-Canadian
boundary."
```

3. Check to see that your language is not too informal.

4. Check all titles of works to make sure that these rules have been followed:

    - You have capitalized the first and last words and all other words except *a, an,* and *the;* coordinating conjunctions; and prepositions that have fewer than five letters.

    - You have punctuated them properly.

5. Check every sentence to make sure that it has an end mark. If the sentence ends with a parenthetical citation, make sure that the citation appears before the end mark. In the case of a long, indented quotation, the citation should follow the end mark.

6. Check every quotation in the body of the text to make sure that it begins and ends with quotation marks. Make sure that quotations within quotations in the body of the text are enclosed in single quotation marks. If a quotation is more than four lines long, it should be set off from the text and indented without quotation marks.

7. Check to see that you have used points of ellipsis properly in edited quotations. (See page 65.)

Proofreading a Research Report (cont.)

8. Make sure that every quotation, summary, or paraphrase is followed by a parenthetical citation. Make sure that every citation corresponds to an entry in the Works Cited list.

9. Check every quotation against your note cards to make sure that it is accurate.

Preparing Your Final Manuscript

After proofreading, you need to prepare your final manuscript. A recommended manuscript form for research reports is described on the next two pages. You may also wish to refer to the sample research report on pages 39–45.

After preparing the final manuscript, proofread it one last time. Mark any corrections neatly on the manuscript, using the proofreading symbols shown in the chart on page 100. If a page contains more than three corrections, consider creating a new final page.

Finally, collect all the parts of the report that your teacher wishes to see—the report itself, including the Works Cited list, and possibly your final outline, your note cards, and your bibliography cards. Congratulations! You have just finished your research report.

Reflecting on Your Writing Process

Think about your experience of writing your report while it is still fresh in your mind. If you reflect now, you may think of some ways to save yourself time as you work on other research reports. In your journal, answer questions such as, What have I learned? What parts of the research process were easiest or most difficult for me? What would I do differently next time?

Guidelines for Manuscript Form: Research Reports

1. **General guidelines/type of paper.** If possible, type or word-process your report. Use high-quality white, unlined 8½″ × 11″ paper. Do not use colored paper, transparent paper, onionskin paper, or odd typefaces, such as script. For information on using word-processing programs for research reports, see Appendix A on pages 103–104.

   If you must write your report by hand, print or use cursive writing, whichever is neater. Use lined paper, write on only one side of each sheet, and follow the same format guidelines that you would follow when typing or word processing.

2. **Margins.** Use one-inch margins at the top, sides, and bottom of the page.

3. **Name and page numbers.** Include your last name, a space, and the page number at the top of each page of the report. The name and page number should appear one-half inch from the top edge of the paper, beginning at the right margin. Number the pages of the report and the Works Cited list continuously, using Arabic numerals (1, 2, 3, and so on). Do not precede the page numbers with the word *page* or any abbreviation of it, such as *p.* or *pg.*

4. **Spacing.** Double-space the entire report, including headings, titles, quotations, and text paragraphs.

5. **Heading.** At the left margin of the first page, drop down one inch from the top edge of the paper and type, on separate lines, your complete name, your teacher's name, the name of your class, and the complete date in this form: 12 November 2000. Double-space between the lines.

6. **Title.** On the line following the date, center the title of your report. Use uppercase and lowercase letters, not all capitals, and underline only those words, such as the titles of long works, that you would underline in the body of your report. Double-space between the date and the title and between the title and the first paragraph of the report.

Guidelines for Manuscript Form: Research Reports (cont.)

7. **Indentions.** Indent the first line of each text paragraph five spaces from the left margin.

8. **Quotations.** See the guidelines for quotations on pages 76–77.

9. **Paragraphing.** Do not leave a single line of a paragraph at the bottom or the top of a page.

10. **Works Cited list.** On the first Works Cited page, after your last name and the page number, drop down an additional one-half inch to a position one inch from the top edge of the paper, and center the title "Works Cited." Do not underline the title or enclose it in quotation marks.

11. **Placement and spacing of Works Cited entries.** Double-space after the title "Works Cited" and begin the first Works Cited entry.

    Double-space and alphabetize all the Works Cited entries. Entries should be alphabetized by their first words, whether the words are parts of titles or of persons' names. If an entry begins with a title, skip any initial article (*a, an,* or *the*) when alphabetizing.

    Begin the first line of each Works Cited entry at the left margin. Indent additional lines five spaces.

12. **Binding and presentation.** Do not staple your research report, and do not use rubber bands. Follow the instructions for binding and presentation given by your teacher. Most teachers will ask that you fasten the pages together with a paper clip.

13. **Final outline.** If your teacher asks you to submit a final outline along with your research report, use one of the formats shown in the sample outlines on pages 71–72. In your final outline, however, replace your statement of controlling purpose with your thesis statement.

Proofreading Symbols

N̶orth of Mexico	Make lowercase.
President jefferson	Capitalize.
a fine t̶h̶i̶n̶g̶ (idea)	Replace.
this t̶h̶i̶s̶ time	Delete.
thier	Transpose.
1, 2 or 3	Add a comma.
Lets go.	Add an apostrophe.
Welcome, friends	Add a period.
They are leaving.	Add letters or words.

Computers and the Research Report

If you have access to a personal computer at home or at school, consider using it to prepare your research report. The following are some ways you can use a personal computer in the various stages of the research process:

1. **Finding sources.** Many libraries have computerized catalogs that can help you to find sources. You can also use a personal computer to find information directly (see items 2 and 3 below).

2. **Using commercial on-line services.** When you use your computer to communicate with another computer, you are working on-line. On-line resources include a number of commercial services that are valuable sources of information. These services offer current facts and news; on-line encyclopedias; access to abstracts or full versions of periodical articles, reports, and government documents; homework assistance; tutoring; classes in many subjects; and research assistance. A few of the on-line services offer connections to libraries and museums, including the Library of Congress and the Smithsonian Institution in Washington, D.C. To use an on-line service, you need either a computer with a modem linked to a telephone line or a television set with an Internet-ready box. Your school's computer lab or resource center may be linked to a commercial on-line service.

3. **Using computer networks.** Some school districts and states have special education computer networks. The TENET, or Texas Education Network, is one example. This network is connected to the Internet, a vast network of computers that connects businesses, universities, and government research centers around the world. With a computer that is linked to the Internet, you can have access to a huge number of information sources. For example, sites on the World Wide Web—one of the Internet's most popular resources— can be a good source of up-to-the-minute information. Your school's

computer lab or resource center may be linked to the Internet or to other state or local networks.

4. **Using CD-ROMs.** If your computer has a CD-ROM drive, you will be able to use some of the many resource materials—from timetables of history and science to encyclopedias to the works of Shakespeare—that are available on CD-ROM. See your local computer dealer about purchasing such discs, or see if your school or community library has a CD-ROM collection.

5. **Preparing computerized bibliography cards and note cards.** You can use database or hypertext programs to prepare note cards and bibliography cards. The advantage of preparing note cards and bibliography cards with such programs is that you can sort the cards automatically, in alphabetical or numerical order, according to any element in them, such as the names of authors or editors, the guidelines, or the source numbers.

6. **Using documentation software.** Several programs are now available that generate bibliographies, Works Cited lists, endnotes, and footnotes automatically, and some word-processing programs have built-in documentation features. However, before you use such a program, make sure that it follows the style that is specified in this book—the style described in the *MLA Handbook for Writers of Research Papers.*

7. **Using outlining software.** Many word-processing programs have built-in outlining features. Separate outlining programs are also available. However, be careful that any program that you use creates outlines in the form described in this book or in a form acceptable to your teacher.

8. **Creating graphics.** You can, of course, use a computer to prepare graphics for your research report. Excellent programs exist for drawing, for creating charts and tables, for creating graphs of all kinds, and for mapping.

Abbreviations for Use in Research Reports

Dates and Geographic Names

See a dictionary or the *MLA Handbook for Writers of Research Papers* for abbreviations of days, months, and geographic names.

Publishers

When including publishers' names in Works Cited entries, footnotes, or endnotes, leave out articles (*a, an, the*), abbreviations of business entities (*Co., Inc., Ltd.*), and words that indicate the business that the publishers are in (*Books, House, Press, Publishers*). However, use the abbreviations *U* for "University" and *P* for "Press" in Works Cited entries for university-press publications, as in *MIT P, U of Texas P, U of Puerto Rico P,* and *Cambridge UP.*

Use the following accepted shortened forms of publishers' names. If a publishing-house name consists of a person's name (Jeremy P. Tarcher, Inc.), then use the last name as the shortened form (Tarcher). If the publisher does not appear in the following list or if the name of the publishing house is not a person's name, consult the *MLA Handbook for Writers of Research Papers,* use an abbreviation of your own that clearly identifies the publisher, or give the publisher's name in full, except for the kinds of words and abbreviations described above.

Abrams	Harry N. Abrams, Inc.	ALA	American Library Association
Allyn	Allyn and Bacon, Inc.	Appleton	Appleton-Century-Crofts
Ballantine	Ballantine Books, Inc.	Bantam	Bantam Books, Inc.
Barnes	Barnes and Noble Books	Basic	Basic Books
Bobbs	The Bobbs-Merrill Co., Inc.	Clarendon	Clarendon Press

Dell	Dell Publishing Co., Inc.	Dodd	Dodd, Mead and Co.
Doubleday	Doubleday and Co., Inc.	Dover	Dover Publications, Inc.
Dutton	E. P. Dutton, Inc.	Funk	Funk and Wagnalls, Inc.
GPO	Government Printing Office	Harcourt	Harcourt Brace Jovanovich, Inc.
Harper	Harper and Row, Publishers, Inc., or HarperCollins Publishers, Inc.	Holt	Holt, Rinehart, and Winston, Inc.
Houghton	Houghton Mifflin Co.	Knopf	Alfred A. Knopf, Inc.
Lippincott	J. B. Lippincott Co.	Little	Little, Brown and Co.
McDougal	McDougal Littell Inc.	McGraw	McGraw-Hill, Inc.
Macmillan	Macmillan Publishing Co., Inc.	MLA	The Modern Language Association of America
Norton	W. W. Norton and Co., Inc.	Penguin	Penguin Books, Inc.
Pocket	Pocket Books	Prentice	Prentice-Hall, Inc.
Putnam's	G. P. Putnam's Sons	Rand	Rand McNally and Co.
Random	Random House, Inc.	St. Martin's	St. Martin's Press, Inc.
Scott	Scott, Foresman and Co.	Simon	Simon and Schuster, Inc.
Twayne	Twayne Publishers	Viking	The Viking Press, Inc.

Sacred Works and Literary Works

For abbreviations of parts of the Bible and other scriptures, consult a dictionary. For standard abbreviations of works by Shakespeare and other classic works of literature, see the *MLA Handbook for Writers of Research Papers.*

Other Abbreviations for Use in Documentation

The following abbreviations, in addition to the ones given on the preceding pages, are commonly used in documentation.

abr.	abridged	ch.	chapter
chs.	chapters	col.	column
cols.	columns	comp.	compiled by, compiler

cond.	conducted by, conductor	dir.	directed by, director
ed.	edited by, editor, edition	eds.	editors, editions
et al.	*et alii, et aliae* ("and others")	fig.	figure
fwd.	foreword by, foreword	illus.	illustrated by, illustrator, illustration
introd.	introduced by, introduction	n.d.	no date
no.	number	n.p.	no place, no publisher
P	Press	p.	page
par.	paragraph	pp.	pages
qtd.	quoted	rev.	revised by, revision, review
rpt.	reprinted by, reprint	sc.	scene
sec.	section	ser.	series
trans.	translated by, translator, translation	U	University
vol.	volume	vers.	version
writ.	written by, writer	vols.	volumes

Forms for Working Bibliography and Works Cited Entries

The following are some basic forms for bibliographic entries. Use these forms on the bibliography cards that make up your working bibliography and in the Works Cited list that appears at the end of your report.

Whole Books

The following models can also be used for reports and pamphlets.

A. One author

Ruiz, Ramón Eduardo. <u>Triumphs and Tragedy: A History of the Mexican People</u>. New York: Norton, 1992.

B. Two authors

Applewhite, Harriet B., and Darline G. Levy. <u>Women and Politics in the Age of the Democratic Revolution</u>. Ann Arbor: U of Michigan P, 1990.

C. Three authors

Demko, George J., Jerome Agel, and Eugene Boe. <u>Why in the World: Adventures in Geography</u>. New York: Anchor-Doubleday, 1992.

D. Four or more authors

The abbreviation *et al.* means "and others." Use *et al.* instead of listing all the authors.

Beringer, Richard E., et al. <u>Why the South Lost the Civil War</u>. Athens: U of Georgia P, 1986.

E. No author identified

Literary Market Place: The Directory of the American
    Book Publishing Industry. 1997 ed. New York:
    Bowker, 1996.

F. An editor, but no single author

Nabokov, Peter, ed. Native American Testimony: A
    Chronicle of Indian-White Relations from Prophecy
    to the Present, 1492-1992. New York: Viking-
    Penguin, 1991.

G. Two or three editors

Harrison, Maureen, and Steve Gilbert, eds. Landmark
    Decisions of the United States Supreme Court.
    Beverly Hills: Excellent, 1991.

H. Four or more editors

The abbreviation *et al.* means "and others." Use *et al.* instead of listing all the editors.

McFarlan, Donald, et al., eds. The Guinness Book of
    Records 1992. New York: Facts on File, 1991.

I. An author and a translator

Levi, Primo. Survival in Auschwitz: The Nazi Assault on
    Humanity. Trans. Stuart Woolf. New York: Collier-
    Macmillan, 1987.

J. An author, a translator, and an editor

Capellanus, Andreas. The Art of Courtly Love. Abr. ed.
    Trans. John J. Parry. Ed. Frederick W. Locke. New
    York: Ungar, 1976.

K. An edition other than the first

Janson, H. W., and Anthony F. Janson. History of Art
    for Young People. 4th ed. New York: Abrams, 1992.

L. A book or monograph that is part of a series

> LaRusso, Carol Spenard, comp. <u>The Green Thoreau</u>.
>   Classic Wisdom Ser. San Rafael: New World, 1992.

M. A multivolume work

If you have used only one volume of a multivolume work, cite only that volume.

> Kimball, Warren F., ed. <u>Churchill and Roosevelt: The</u>
>   <u>Complete Correspondence</u>. Vol. 3. Princeton:
>   Princeton UP, 1984. 3 vols.

If you have used more than one volume of a multivolume work, cite the entire work.

> Kimball, Warren F., ed. <u>Churchill and Roosevelt: The</u>
>   <u>Complete Correspondence</u>. 3 vols. Princeton:
>   Princeton UP, 1984.

N. A volume with its own title that is part of a multivolume work with a different title

> Durant, Will, and Ariel Durant. <u>Rousseau and</u>
>   <u>Revolution: A History of Civilization in France,</u>
>   <u>England, and Germany from 1756, and in the</u>
>   <u>Remainder of Europe from 1715, to 1789</u>. New York:
>   Simon, 1967. Vol. 10 of <u>The Story of Civilization</u>.
>   11 vols. 1935-75.

O. A republished book or a literary work available in several editions

Give the date of the original publication after the title. Then give complete publication information, including the date, for the edition that you have used.

> Steinbeck, John. <u>The Grapes of Wrath</u>. 1939. New York:
>   Penguin, 1976.

P. A government publication

Give the name of the government (country or state). Then give the department, followed by the agency if applicable. Next give the title, followed by the author if known. Then give the publication information. The publisher of U.S. government documents is usually the Government Printing Office, or GPO.

United States. Dept. of Education. Office of Educational
        Research and Improvement. <u>OERI Publications Guide</u>.
        By Lance Ferderer. Washington: GPO, 1990.

---. ---. ---. Educational Resources Information
        Center. <u>Recent Department of Education</u>
        <u>Publications in ERIC</u>. Washington: GPO, 1992.

Parts of Books

A. A poem, short story, essay, or chapter in a collection of works by one author

Cather, Willa. "Joseph and His Brothers." <u>Cather:</u>
        <u>Stories, Poems, and Other Writings</u>. Comp. Sharon
        O'Brien. New York: Viking, 1992. 859-71.

B. A poem, short story, essay, or chapter in a collection of works by several authors

West, Paul. "Pelé." <u>The Norton Book of Sports</u>. Ed.
        George Plimpton. New York: Norton, 1992. 308.

C. A novel or play in an anthology

Simmons, Alexander. <u>Sherlock Holmes and the Hands of</u>
        <u>Othello</u>. <u>Black Thunder: An Anthology of</u>
        <u>Contemporary African American Drama</u>. Ed. William
        B. Branch. New York: Mentor, 1992. 359-415.

D. An introduction, preface, foreword, or afterword written by the author(s) of a work

Pinson, Linda, and Jerry Jinnett. Dedication. <u>The Woman</u>
        <u>Entrepreneur</u>. Ed. Pinson and Jinnett. Tustin: Out
        of Your Mind, 1992. iii.

E. An introduction, preface, foreword, or afterword written by someone other than the author(s) of a work

```
Coles, Robert. Foreword. No Place to Be: Voices of
    Homeless Children. By Judith Berck. Boston:
    Houghton, 1992. 1-4.
```

F. Cross-references

If you have used more than one work from a collection, you may give a complete entry for the collection. Then, in the separate entries for the works, you can refer to the entry for the whole collection by using the editor's last name or, if you have listed more than one work by that editor, the editor's last name and a shortened version of the title.

```
French, Warren, ed. A Companion to The Grapes of Wrath.
    New York: Viking, 1963.

---. "What Did John Steinbeck Know About the 'Okies'?"
    French, Companion 51-53.

Steinbeck, John. Their Blood Is Strong. San Francisco:
    Lubin, 1938. Rpt. in French, Companion 53-92.
```

G. A reprinted article or essay (one previously published somewhere else)

If a work that appears in a collection first appeared in another place, give complete information for the original publication, followed by *Rpt. in* and complete information for the collection.

```
Meier, August. "Toward a Reinterpretation of Booker T.
    Washington." Journal of Southern History 23
    (1957): 220-27. Rpt. in The Making of Black
    America: Essays in Negro Life and History. Ed.
    August Meier and Elliott Rudwick. Vol. 2. New
    York: Atheneum, 1969. 125-30.
```

Magazines, Journals, Newspapers, and Encyclopedias

A. An article in a magazine, journal, or newspaper

```
Smith, Shelley. "Baseball's Forgotten Pioneers." Sports
     Illustrated 30 Mar. 1992: 72.

Schwartz, Felice N. "Women as a Business Imperative."
     Harvard Business Review 70.2 (1992): 105-13.

"Kozyrev's Mission to Washington." Editorial. Boston
     Globe 14 June 1992: 78.
```

If no author is identified, begin with the article's title. If an author is identified, begin with the author's name followed by the article's title. When an article continues on a page that does not follow immediately after its first page, use a plus sign (+) after the number of the page on which it begins.

B. An article in an encyclopedia or other alphabetically organized reference work

Give the title of the article, the name of the reference work, and the year of the edition.

```
"Zuni." Encyclopaedia Britannica: Micropaedia. 1992 ed.
```

C. A review

```
Gutiérrez, David G. Rev. of Conquests and Historical
     Identities in California, 1769-1936, by Lisbeth
     Haas. American Historical Review 101.5 (1996):
     1610-11.
```

If the review is unsigned, begin with *Rev. of* and the title.

Media and Other Sources

A. An interview you have conducted or letter you have received

```
Jackson, Jesse. Personal interview [or Letter to the
    author]. 15 July 1992.
```

B. A film

```
Glory. Screenplay by Kevin Jarre. Dir. Edward Zwick.
    Perf. Matthew Broderick, Morgan Freeman, and Denzel
    Washington. TriStar, 1989.
```

C. A work of art (painting, photograph, sculpture)

```
Catlin, George. Four Bears, Second Chief, in Full
    Dress. National Museum of American Art,
    Smithsonian Institution, Washington.
```

D. A television or a radio program

Give the episode name (if applicable) and the series or program name. Include any information that you have about the program's writer and director. Then give the network, the local station, the city, and the date the program aired.

```
"A Desert Blooming." Living Wild. Writ. Marshall
    Riggan. Dir. Harry L. Gorden. PBS. WTTW, Chicago.
    29 Apr. 1984.
```

E. A musical composition

```
Chopin, Frédéric. Waltz in A-flat major, op. 42.
```

F. A sound recording (compact disc, LP, or audiocassette)

If the recording is not a compact disc, include *LP* or *Audiocassette* before the manufacturer's name.

```
Guthrie, Woody. "Do-Re-Me." Dust Bowl Ballads.
    Rounder, 1988.
```

G. A lecture, speech, or address

Give the name of the speaker followed by the title of the speech (if applicable) or the kind of speech (*Lecture, Introduction, Address*). Then give the event, the place, and the date.

```
Benjamin, John. Address. First Annual Abolitionist
    March and Rally. Boston. 18 July 1992.
```

Electronic Media

Because the number of electronic information sources is increasing rapidly, please refer to the most current edition of the MLA Handbook for Writers of Research Papers *if you need more complete information. You can also refer to the page "MLA Style" on the Modern Language Association Web site <http://www.mla.org>.*

Portable databases (CD-ROMs, DVDs, laser discs, diskettes, and videocassettes)

These products contain fixed information (information that cannot be changed unless a new version is produced and released). Citing them in a research report is similar to citing printed sources. You should include the following information:

- Name of the author (if applicable)
- Title of the part of the work used (if applicable) underlined or in quotation marks
- Title of the product or database (underlined)
- Publication medium (CD-ROM, DVD, laser disc, diskette, or videocassette)
- Edition, release, or version (if applicable)
- City of publication
- Name of publisher
- Year of publication

If you cannot find some of this information, cite what is available.

> Boyer, Paul S., et al. "Troubled Agriculture." <u>The Enduring Vision: A History of the American People, Interactive Edition</u>. CD-ROM. Vers. 1.1. Lexington: Heath, 1993.
>
> "Steinbeck's Dust Bowl Saga." <u>Our Times Multimedia Encyclopedia of the 20th Century</u>. CD-ROM. 1996 ed. Redwood City: Vicarious, 1995.
>
> "The Cold War Comes Home: Hollywood Blacklists the Kahn Family." <u>American Stories</u>. Laser disc. McDougal, 1998.
>
> <u>Eyes on the Prize: America's Civil Rights Years</u>. Prod. Blackside. 6 episodes. Videocassettes. PBS Video, 1986.

On-Line Sources

The many sources on the Internet include scholarly projects, reference databases, articles in periodicals, and professional and personal sites. Not all sites are equally reliable, and therefore material gathered from the Internet should be evaluated carefully. Entries for on-line sources in the Works Cited list should contain as much of the information listed below as is available.

- Name of the author, editor, compiler, or translator, accompanied by an abbreviation, such as *ed., comp.,* or *trans.,* if applicable
- Title of the material. Use quotation marks for poems, short stories, articles, and similar short works. Underline the title of a book.
- Publication information for any print version of the source
- Title (underlined) of the scholarly project, database, periodical, or professional or personal site. For a professional or personal site with no title, add a description such as *Home page* (with no underlining or quotation marks).
- Name of the editor of the scholarly project or database
- For a journal, the volume number, issue number, or other identifying number
- Date of electronic publication, latest update, or posting
- For a work from a subscription service, the name of the service and—if a library is the subscriber—the name of the library and the town or state where it is located
- Range or total number of pages, paragraphs, or other sections if they are numbered
- Name of any institution or organization that sponsors or is associated with the Web site
- Date the source was accessed
- Electronic address, or URL, of the source. For a subscription service, use the URL of the service's main page (if known) or the keyword assigned to the service.

A. Scholarly project

<u>Martha Heasley Cox Center for Steinbeck Studies</u>. Sept.
    1999. San Jose State U. 30 Sept. 1999
    <http://www.sjsu.edu/depts/steinbec/srchome.html>.

B. Professional site

<u>American Council of Learned Societies Home Page</u>. 1998.
    Amer. Council of Learned Societies. 30 Sept. 1999
    <http://www.acls.org/jshome.htm>.

C. Personal site

Stephan, Ed. <u>John Steinbeck: The California Novels</u>.
     30 Sept. 1999 <http://www.ac.wwu.edu/~stephan/
     Steinbeck/index.html>.

D. Book

Mabbutt, J. A., and Andrew W. Wilson, eds. <u>Social and
     Environmental Aspects of Desertification.</u> Tokyo:
     United Nations UP, 1980. 20 Jan. 2000
     <http://www.unu.edu/unupress/unupbooks/80127e/
     80127E00.htm>.

E. Article in reference database

"Dust Bowl." <u>Encyclopaedia Britannica Online.</u> Vers.
     99.1. Encyclopaedia Britannica. 1 Oct. 1999
     <http://www.eb.com:180/bol/topic?eu=32140&sctn=1>.

F. Article in journal

Park, Tai H. "Morality, Individual Responsibility,
     and the Law." <u>Philosophy and Literature</u> 22.1
     (1998). 6 Oct. 1999<http://www.press.jhu.edu/
     journals/philosophy_and_literature/v022/
     22.1park.html>.

G. Article in magazine

Chiles, James R. "Bang! Went the Doors of Every Bank in
     America." <u>Smithsonian</u> Apr. 1997. Abstract. 1 Oct.
     1999<http://www.smithsonianmag.si.edu/smithsonian/
     issues97/apr/97/banks.html>.

H. Work from a subscription service

"Dust Bowl." <u>Compton's Encyclopedia Online</u>. Vers. 3.0.
     1998. America Online. 5 Oct. 1999. Keyword:
     Compton's.

Hinton, Rebecca. "Steinbeck's <u>The Grapes of Wrath</u>."
     <u>Explicator</u> 56 (Winter 1998): 101-103.
     <u>WilsonSelect</u>. FirstSearch. Evanston Public Lib.,
     IL. 4 Oct. 1999 <http://firstsearch.oclc.org>.

Alternative Documentation Styles

The documentation style suggested in this book, which involves parenthetical citations and a Works Cited list, is recommended in the *MLA Handbook for Writers of Research Papers* and is widely used for work in languages, literature, the arts, and the humanities throughout the English-speaking world. Another common type of documentation involves the use of endnotes or footnotes.

Endnote and Footnote Styles

Some people prefer endnotes or footnotes to parenthetical citations because they do not clutter the text of the research report. Instead of a citation, what appears in the text is a number placed after a sentence and above the line, as in the following example:

```
Colonel Shaw's mother is said to have cried from

happiness on seeing her son at the head of the all-

African-American 54th Massachusetts.⁵
```

The number that is placed above the line is called a **superscript.** Throughout the paper, information taken from sources marked with such superscripts. Each superscript refers the reader to a note that appears either at the bottom of that page or at the end of the report. If the note appears at the bottom of the page, it is called a **footnote.** If it appears at the end of the report, it is called an **endnote.** Footnotes are no longer popular because they clutter the report. Most writers who use notes instead of parenthetical citations prefer endnotes. The following is a sample endnote or footnote:

    ⁵ `Shelby Foote, `*`Fredericksburg to Meridian`*` (New York:`
`Random, 1963), vol. 2 of `*`The Civil War: A Narrative`*`, 3`
`vols. (1958-74) 697.`

An endnote or footnote differs from a working bibliography or Works Cited entry in the following ways:

1. The first line of a working bibliography or Works Cited entry begins at the left margin. The first line of an endnote or footnote is indented five spaces.

2. Run-over lines of a working bibliography or Works Cited entry are indented five spaces. Run-over lines of an endnote or footnote begin at the left margin.

3. A working bibliography or Works Cited entry does not have a super-script at the beginning. An endnote or footnote does.

4. The name at the beginning of a working bibliography or Works Cited entry is reversed for alphabetizing. In an endnote or footnote, the name is given in its normal order.

5. A working bibliography or Works Cited entry has three main parts, each of which ends with a period: the name, the title, and the publication information. An endnote or footnote has four main parts, only the last of which ends with a period: the name, the title, the publication information, and the page number(s).

6. The publication information in an endnote or footnote is enclosed in parentheses; in a working bibliography or Works Cited entry, it is not.

For proper placement of endnotes and footnotes, see the sample research report on pages 129–135. The following pages give sample forms for endnotes and footnotes.

Forms for Endnotes or Footnotes

Whole Books

The following models can also be used for reports and pamphlets.

A. One author

[1] Ramón Eduardo Ruiz, <u>Triumphs and Tragedy: A History of the Mexican People</u> (New York: Norton, 1992) 14.

B. Two authors

[2] Harriet B. Applewhite and Darline G. Levy, <u>Women and Politics in the Age of the Democratic Revolution</u> (Ann Arbor: U of Michigan P, 1990) 63.

C. Three authors

[3] George J. Demko, Jerome Agel, and Eugene Boe, <u>Why in the World: Adventures in Geography</u> (New York: Anchor-Doubleday, 1992) 15-16.

D. Four or more authors

The abbreviation *et al.* means "and others." Use *et al.* instead of listing all the authors.

[4] Richard E. Beringer et al., <u>Why the South Lost the Civil War</u> (Athens: U of Georgia P, 1986) 56.

E. No author identified

[5] <u>Literary Market Place: The Directory of the American Book Publishing Industry</u>, 1997 ed. (New York: Bowker, 1996) 1673.

F. An editor, but no single author

[6] Peter Nabokov, ed., <u>Native American Testimony: A Chronicle of Indian-White Relations from Prophecy to the Present, 1492-1992</u> (New York: Viking-Penguin, 1991) 101.

G. Two or three editors

7 Maureen Harrison and Steve Gilbert, eds., <u>Landmark Decisions of the United States Supreme Court</u> (Beverly Hills: Excellent, 1991) 106.

H. Four or more editors

The abbreviation *et al.* means "and others." Use *et al.* instead of listing all the editors.

8 Donald McFarlan et al., eds., <u>The Guinness Book of Records 1992</u> (New York: Facts on File, 1991) 99.

I. An author and a translator

9 Primo Levi, <u>Survival in Auschwitz: The Nazi Assault on Humanity</u>, trans. Stuart Woolf (New York: Collier-Macmillan, 1987) 115.

J. An author, a translator, and an editor

10 Andreas Capellanus, <u>The Art of Courtly Love</u>, abr. ed., trans. John J. Parry, ed. Frederick W. Locke (New York: Ungar, 1976) 42.

K. An edition of a book other than the first

11 H. W. Janson and Anthony F. Janson, <u>History of Art for Young People</u>, 4th ed. (New York: Abrams, 1992) 45.

L. A book or monograph that is part of a series

12 Carol Spenard LaRusso, comp., <u>The Green Thoreau</u>, Classic Wisdom Ser. (San Rafael: New World, 1992) 47.

M. A multivolume work

If you are referring to a particular place in one volume, use this form:

13 Warren F. Kimball, ed., <u>Churchill and Roosevelt: The Complete Correspondence</u>, vol. 3 (Princeton: Princeton UP, 1984) 228.

Endnotes and footnotes that refer to entire works are quite rare. However, if you are referring to an entire multivolume work, use the following form, with no page number:

14 Warren F. Kimball, ed., <u>Churchill and Roosevelt: The Complete Correspondence</u>, 3 vols. (Princeton: Princeton UP, 1984).

N. A volume with its own title that is part of a multivolume work with a different title

¹⁵ Will Durant and Ariel Durant, <u>Rousseau and Revolution: A History of Civilization in France, England, and Germany from 1756, and in the Remainder of Europe from 1715, to 1789</u> (New York: Simon, 1967), vol. 10 of <u>The Story of Civilization</u>, 11 vols. (1935-75) 18.

O. A republished book or a literary work available in several editions

Give the date of the original publication, followed by a semicolon, then give the place of publication and the date of the edition that you have used.

¹⁶ John Steinbeck, <u>The Grapes of Wrath</u> (1939; New York: Penguin, 1976) 339.

P. A government publication

Give the name of the government (country or state). Then give the department, followed by the agency if applicable. Next give the title, followed by the author if known. Then give the publication information. The publisher of U.S. government documents is usually the Government Printing Office, or GPO.

¹⁷ United States, Dept. of Education, Office of Educational Research and Improvement, <u>OERI Publications Guide</u>, by Lance Ferderer (Washington: GPO, 1990) 27.

¹⁸ ---, ---, ---, Educational Resources Information Center, <u>Recent Department of Education Publications in ERIC</u> (Washington: GPO, 1992) 162.

Parts of Books

A. A poem, short story, essay, or chapter in a collection of works by one author

¹⁹ Willa Cather, "Joseph and His Brothers," <u>Cather: Stories, Poems, and Other Writings</u>, comp. Sharon O'Brien (New York: Viking, 1992) 860.

B.   A poem, short story, essay, or chapter in a collection of works by several authors

20 Paul West, "Pelé," <u>The Norton Book of Sports</u>, ed. George Plimpton (New York: Norton, 1992) 308.

C.   A novel or play in an anthology

21 Alexander Simmons, <u>Sherlock Holmes and the Hands of Othello</u>, <u>Black Thunder: An Anthology of Contemporary African American Drama</u>, ed. William B. Branch (New York: Mentor, 1992) 411.

D.   An introduction, preface, foreword, or afterword written by the author(s) of a work

22 Linda Pinson and Jerry Jinnett, dedication, <u>The Woman Entrepreneur</u>, ed. Pinson and Jinnett (Tustin: Out of Your Mind, 1992) iii.

E.   An introduction, preface, foreword, or afterword written by someone other than the author(s) of a work

23 Robert Coles, foreword, <u>No Place to Be: Voices of Homeless Children</u>, by Judith Berck (Boston: Houghton, 1992) 2.

F.   A reprinted article or essay (one previously published somewhere else)

If a work that appears in a collection first appeared in another place, give complete information for the original publication, followed by *rpt. in* and complete information for the collection.

24 August Meier, "Toward a Reinterpretation of Booker T. Washington," <u>Journal of Southern History</u> 23 (1957): 220-27, rpt. in <u>The Making of Black America: Essays in Negro Life and History</u>, ed. August Meier and Elliot Rudwick, vol. 2 (New York: Atheneum, 1969) 125-30.

Magazines, Journals, Newspapers, and Encyclopedias

A. An article in a magazine, journal, or newspaper

25 Shelley Smith, "Baseball's Forgotten Pioneers," Sports Illustrated 30 Mar. 1992: 72.

26 Felice N. Schwartz, "Women as a Business Imperative," Harvard Business Review 70.2 (1992): 105-13.

27 "Kozyrev's Mission to Washington," editorial, Boston Globe 14 June 1992: 78.

If no author is identified, begin with the article's title. If an author is identified, begin with the author's name followed by the article's title. When an article continues on a page that does not follow its first page immediately, use a plus sign (+) after the number of the page on which it begins.

B. An article in an encyclopedia or other alphabetically organized reference work

Give the title of the article, the name of the reference work, and the year of the edition.

28 "Zuni," Encyclopaedia Britannica: Micropaedia, 1992 ed.

C. A review

29 David G. Gutiérrez, rev. of Conquests and Historical Identities in California, 1769-1936, by Lisbeth Haas, American Historical Review 101.5 (1996): 1610-11.

If the review is unsigned, begin with *Rev. of* and the title.

Media and Other Sources

A. An interview you have conducted or letter you have received

[30] Jesse Jackson, personal interview [*or* letter to the author], 15 July 1992.

B. A film

[31] Glory, screenplay by Kevin Jarre, dir. Edward Zwick, perf. Matthew Broderick, Morgan Freeman, and Denzel Washington, TriStar, 1989.

C. A work of art (painting, photograph, sculpture)

[32] George Catlin, Four Bears, Second Chief, in Full Dress, National Museum of American Art, Smithsonian Institution, Washington.

D. A television or a radio program

Give the episode name (if applicable) and the series or program name. Include any information that you have about the program's writer and director. Then give the network, the local station, the city, and the date the program aired.

[33] "A Desert Blooming," Living Wild, writ. Marshall Riggan, dir. Harry L. Gorden, PBS, WTTW, Chicago, 29 Apr. 1984.

E. A musical composition

[34] Frédéric Chopin, Waltz in A-flat major, op. 42.

F. A sound recording (compact disc, LP, or audiocassette)

If the recording is not a compact disc, include *LP* or *audiocassette* before the manufacturer's name.

[35] Woody Guthrie, "Do-Re-Me," Dust Bowl Ballads, Rounder, 1988.

G. A lecture, speech, or address

Give the name of the speaker followed by the title of the speech (if applicable) or the kind of speech (*lecture, introduction, address*). Then give the event, the place, and the date.

[36] John Benjamin, address, First Annual Abolitionist March and Rally, Boston, 18 July 1992.

Electronic Media

Because the number of electronic information sources is increasing rapidly, please refer to the most current edition of the MLA Handbook for Writers of Research Papers *if you need more complete information. You can also refer to the page "MLA Style" on the Modern Language Association Web site <http://www.mla.org>.*

Portable databases (CD-ROMs, DVDs, laser discs, diskettes, and videocassettes)

These products contain fixed information (information that cannot be changed unless a new version is produced and released). Citing them in a research report is similar to citing printed sources. You should include the following information:

- Name of the author (if applicable)
- Title of the part of the work used (if applicable), underlined or in quotation marks
- Title of the product or database (underlined)
- Publication medium (CD-ROM, DVD, laser disc, diskette, or videocassette)
- Edition, release, or version (if applicable)
- City of publication
- Name of publisher
- Year of publication

If you cannot find some of this information, cite what is available.

[37] Paul S. Boyer et al., "Troubled Agriculture," The Enduring Vision: A History of the American People, Interactive Edition, CD-ROM, vers. 1.1, (Lexington: Heath, 1993).

[38] "Steinbeck's Dust Bowl Saga," Our Times Multimedia Encyclopedia of the 20th Century, CD-ROM, 1996 ed., (Redwood City: Vicarious, 1995).

[39] "The Cold War Comes Home: Hollywood Blacklists the Kahn Family," American Stories, laser disc, McDougal, 1998.

[40] Eyes on the Prize: America's Civil Rights Years, prod. Blackside, 6 episodes, videocassettes, PBS Video, 1986.

On-Line Sources

Because on-line resources may be updated or changed frequently, it is important to include complete information when citing them:

- Name of the author, editor, compiler, or translator, accompanied by an abbreviation, such as *ed., comp.,* or *trans.,* if applicable
- Title of the material, underlined or enclosed in quotation marks as necessary
- Publication information for any print version of the source
- Title of the Web site, underlined
- Name of the editor of the scholarly project or database
- For a journal, the volume number, issue number, or other identifying number
- Date of electronic publication, latest update, or posting
- For a work from a subscription service, the name of the service and—if a library is the subscriber—the name of the library and the town or state where it is located
- Range or number of pages, paragraphs, or other sections if they are numbered
- Name of any institution or organization associated with the Web site
- Date the source was accessed
- Electronic address, or URL, of the source. For a subscription service, use the URL of the service's main page (if known) or the keyword assigned to the service.

41 Martha Heasley Cox Center for Steinbeck Studies. Sept. 1999, San Jose State U, 30 Sept. 1999 <http://www.sjsu.edu/depts/steinbec/srchome.html>.

42 J. A. Mabbutt and Andrew W. Wilson, eds., Social and Environmental Aspects of Desertification (Tokyo: United Nations UP, 1980), 20 Jan. 2000 <http://www.unu.edu/ unupress/unupbooks/80127e/80127E00.htm>.

43 James R. Chiles, "Bang! Went the Doors of Every Bank in America," Smithsonian Apr. 1997, abstract, 1 Oct 1999 <http://www.smithsonianmag.si.edu/smithsonian/issues97/ apr97/banks.html>.

44 "Dust Bowl," Compton's Encyclopedia Online, vers. 3.0, 1998, America Online, 5 Oct. 1999, keyword: Compton's.

For additional information on citing on-line sources, see pages 116–117.

Subsequent References

The first time that you write an endnote or footnote for a work, give a full entry. In subsequent notes, you can give the author's or editor's name by itself:

51 Warren French, "What Did John Steinbeck Know About the 'Okies'?" <u>A Companion to</u> The Grapes of Wrath, ed. French (New York: Viking, 1963) 52.

52 French 53.

If you have cited more than one work by the author or editor, then include shortened forms of the titles in subsequent endnotes or footnotes:

53 French, "What Did" 53.

Other Types of Documentation

Two other documentation styles are in widespread use today. The **author-date system** is widely used in the sciences. This system is similar to parenthetical documentation, but each parenthetical citation includes the date of publication and the page number(s), preceded by *p.* or *pp.*, after the author's or editor's last name.

Wendell Phillips, a leader of the Boston abolition-

ists, had declared, "We have given the sword to the

white man; the time has come to give it to the

black!" (Burchard, 1965, p. 43).

As the following examples show, the Works Cited entries used in the author-date system differ in a number of ways from those used in the parenthetical-documentation system. For details about the preparation of such entries, see the *Publication Manual of the American Psychological Association*.

Burchard, P. (1965). <u>One gallant rush: Robert Gould Shaw and his brave black regiment</u>. New York: St. Martin's Press.

Foote, S. (1958-74). <u>The Civil War: A narrative</u>. (Vols. 1-3). New York: Random House.

Schwartz, F. N. (1992). Women as a business imperative. <u>Harvard Business Review, 70</u> (2), 105-13.

In the **number system** of documentation, each entry in the Works Cited list is numbered with an Arabic numeral (1, 2, 3, and so on). The entries are usually arranged in the order in which the works are cited in the research report. Here are two examples of such entries:

1. Burchard, P. <u>One gallant rush: Robert Gould Shaw and his brave black regiment</u>. New York: St. Martin's Press, 1965.

2. Foote, S. <u>The Civil War: A narrative</u>. 3 vols. New York: Random House, 1958-74.

A parenthetical citation in the text of the research report consists of the number of a Works Cited entry, a comma, the abbreviation *p.* or *pp.*, and the page number(s).

```
Wendell Phillips, a leader of the Boston abolition-

ists, had declared, "We have given the sword to the

white man; the time has come to give it to the

black!" (1, p. 43).
```

Other Style Manuals

The documentation style used in this book is that of the *MLA Handbook for Writers of Research Papers*. Other style manuals that are widely used, especially in social studies and the humanities, include the following:

The Chicago Manual of Style

A Manual for Writers of Term Papers, Theses, and Dissertations, by Kate Turabian

Publication Manual of the American Psychological Association

Michael Maddox
Mr. Mills
History
14 April 2000

This is a sample report done in endnote style. For a page of a report done in footnote style, see page 135.

A History of the Bill of Rights

We, the people of the United States, enjoy freedoms that no other people in the history of the world have experienced. These freedoms are guaranteed in the first ten amendments to the U.S. Constitution, called the Bill of Rights. Today it is easy for us to take these rights for granted, but they were originally a daring experiment in a new kind of government. Former Chief Justice Earl Warren wrote:

> The foundation for "Life, Liberty and the Pursuit of Happiness" resides in the Bill of Rights. [. . .] None of these provisions, of course, was completely original with the Founding Fathers. Each of them was inspired by accumulating knowledge of persecution and human suffering, not only in the colonies and in England, but throughout recorded history wherever one man or a group of men unrestrained have been empowered to control the lives of the people.[1]

Understanding the history that led up to the creation of the Bill of Rights and the freedoms that they provide can help us appreciate our country and its government.

The events that made the Bill of Rights possible began nearly 800 years ago. In 1215, King John of England limited the power of government and granted important liberties to the English people. The rules for this new relationship between the government and the people it governed were spelled out in a document called the Magna Carta, or Great Charter. The Magna Carta prevented the king from becoming a dictator, and it

Note that numbers referring to endnotes are superscripted, or raised above the line.

The topic sentence of this paragraph indicates that the following section of the report will explain the history behind the Bill of Rights. The material in the section is organized chronologically.

129

A superscript is placed outside a closing quotation mark.

became known as a "battle cry against oppression."[2] One important principle that it established was that of no taxation without representation. American colonists would later use this principle in fighting for their independence from England.

Five hundred and sixty years later, the most important event in the development of the Bill of Rights took place. That was the writing of the Virginia Declaration of Rights by George Mason in 1776. Mason felt that it was important for the Virginia Constitution to include a declaration of rights. He wrote this declaration, which included ten articles covering the various rights. The state government accepted all of the articles. Mason then made a copy of the Declaration of Rights and sent it to Thomas Jefferson, who was working on the Declaration of Independence. Jefferson incorporated Mason's ideas into the Declaration of Independence, claiming that "all men [. . .] are endowed [. . .] with certain unalienable Rights."[3]

After the American Revolution, the new citizens of the United States began to abuse their new freedoms. People began taking each other to court to steal property and other wealth. In August 1786, Daniel Shays led a revolt in Massachusetts to stop this practice.[4] Shays and his followers prevented the state courts and the Supreme Court from hearing cases against people who owed money. They freed prisoners and removed the governor from office. The young country "had suffered a very bad scare [. . .] and something had to be done."[5]

A convention was called in Philadelphia to revise the Articles of Confederation, which were the laws that had been drawn up to govern the states as a whole.[6] Fifty-five delegates representing all the states but Rhode Island attended the convention. Instead of revising the Articles of

130

Confederation, though, they drafted the Constitution of the United States. This document set out guidelines for a centralized, or federal, government. Three members of the convention felt so strongly that a Bill of Rights should be included that they refused to sign the Constitution.[7]

By September 19, 1787, the new Constitution was published and was sent to the states for ratification. Nine of the thirteen states were required to ratify the document before it could be accepted. Supporters of the Constitution called themselves Federalists; those who opposed it were Antifederalists. The Antifederalists, who were led by George Mason, said that the Constitution should not be ratified unless it was amended to include a bill of rights. Thomas Jefferson, who was a Federalist, also believed strongly that a bill of rights was "what the people are entitled to against every government on earth, general or particular, and what no just government should refuse."[8]

Most of the states refused to ratify the Constitution without the promise that a bill of rights would be added. George Washington understood this and made it his first priority when he assumed the office of president in April 1789. Congress approved twelve articles of rights, and they were sent to the states for ratification. Three-fourths of the states ratified Articles 3 through 12 by January 15, 1791. These ten amendments, known as the Bill of Rights, became part of the Constitution on December 15, 1791.

These are the rights and freedoms that the amendments of the Bill of Rights guarantee to all Americans:

Amendment 1. Religious and Political Freedom--freedom of religion, speech, peaceable assembly, and the press, as well

The topic sentence of this paragraph indicates that the following section of the report will explain the provisions of the Bill of Rights.

as the right to petition. One of the main reasons the colonists came to New England was to escape religious persecution in England. This amendment was included to protect U.S. citizens from similar oppression.

Amendment 2. Right to Bear Arms--the right of citizens to protect themselves and to stop oppression. Without weapons, the colonists would never have been able to defeat Britain and gain their independence.

Amendment 3. Quartering Troops--the right of controlling how private property is used. This amendment was included because of the British practice of quartering, or housing, its soldiers on private property without the consent of the property owners. This is the only amendment that has never been challenged.[9]

Amendment 4. Search and Seizure--the right to be safe from having private property searched and taken without a good reason and proper authority. This amendment was included because British officials had been allowed to search private property for any reason.

Amendment 5. Rights of Accused Persons--the right to a fair trial, to not be a witness against oneself, to not be tried twice for the same crime, and to not have property taken without proper payment. This amendment also was included as a reaction to abuses the colonists experienced under British rule.

Amendment 6. Right to a Speedy, Public Trial--the right of a person accused in a criminal case to be informed of the charges against him, to be represented by a lawyer, to confront the witnesses against him, and to be tried by an impartial jury. This amendment was a reaction to the British practice of arresting colonists and taking them to Britain for trial.

Amendment 7. Trial by Jury in Civil Cases--the right to a trial by jury in civil cases. This amendment was the result of abuses by dishonest British judges.

Amendment 8. Limits of Fines and Punishments--freedom from excessive fines, bail, or cruel punishment. This amendment was included in response to the punishments the British had inflicted on the colonists.

Amendment 9. Rights of People--the right to freedoms and rights not stated specifically in the Bill of Rights. An example of such a right is the right to privacy.

Amendment 10. Powers of States and People--the right of the states or the people to any powers not specifically given to the U.S. government by the Constitution. This amendment was added because critics of the Constitution feared the power it gave to the central government.

The Bill of Rights was written to ensure the rights of U.S. citizens to be governed justly. We must appreciate these rights and work to preserve them because, as Warren reminded us, the greatest threat to our country comes from the "mindless abandonment of power by the people."[10]

Ending with a quotation is an effective way to conclude a research report.

Notes

[1] Earl Warren, <u>A Republic, If You Can Keep It</u> (New York: Quadrangle, 1972) 110.

[2] "Magna Carta," <u>Encyclopaedia Britannica Online</u>, vers. 99.1, Encyclopaedia Britannica, 7 Apr. 2000 <http://www.eb.com:180/bol/topic?eu=51218&sctn=1#s_top>.

[3] "The Declaration of Independence: A Transcription," <u>The Charters of Freedom</u>, 26 Sep. 1997, Natl. Archives and Records Administration, 7 Apr. 2000 <http://www.nara.gov/exhall/charters/declaration/declaration.html>.

[4] Donald Barr Chidsey, <u>The Birth of the Constitution</u> (New York: Crown, 1964) 15.

[5] Chidsey 17.

[6] Max Farrand, <u>The Framing of the Constitution of the United States</u> (New Haven: Yale UP, 1965) 191.

[7] Farrand 192.

[8] Qtd. in Warren 112.

[9] Warren, 127–128.

[10] Warren 169.

Michael Maddox

Mr. Mills

History

14 April 2000

A History of the Bill of Rights

We, the people of the United States, enjoy freedoms that no other people in the history of the world have experienced. These freedoms are guaranteed in the first ten amendments to the U.S. Constitution, called the Bill of Rights. Today it is easy for us to take these rights for granted, but they were originally a daring experiment in a new kind of government. Former Chief Justice Earl Warren wrote:

> The foundation for "Life, Liberty and the Pursuit of Happiness" resides in the Bill of Rights. [. . .] None of these provisions, of course, was completely original with the Founding Fathers. Each of them was inspired by accumulating knowledge of persecution and human suffering, not only in the colonies and in England, but throughout recorded history wherever one man or a group of men unrestrained have been empowered to control the lives of the people.[1]

Understanding the history that led up to the creation of the Bill of Rights and the freedoms that they provide can help us appreciate our country and its government.

[1] Earl Warren, A Republic, If You Can Keep It (New York: Quadrangle, 1972) 110.

This is the first page of the report that appears on page 129, done in footnote style.

A footnote includes the same information and is done in the same style as an endnote. It appears at the bottom of the page on which the work is cited.

Index